Pindar

Twayne's World Authors Series

Greek Literature

Ruth Scodel, Editor

University of Michigan

TWAS 773

THE CHARIOTEER OF DELPHI (ca. 475 B.C.)
*Photograph courtesy of the Archaeological Receipts Fund
of the Greek Ministry of Culture and Science*

Pindar

By William H. Race

Vanderbilt University

Twayne Publishers • *Boston*

Pindar

William H. Race

Copyright © 1986 by G. K. Hall & Co.
All Rights Reserved
Published by Twayne Publishers
A Division of G. K. Hall & Co.
70 Lincoln Street
Boston, Massachusetts 02111

Copyediting supervised by Lewis DeSimone
Book production by Elizabeth Todesco
Book design by Barbara Anderson

Typeset in 11 pt. Garamond
by Compset, Inc., Beverly, Massachusetts

Printed on permanent/durable acid-free paper
and bound in the United States of America

Library of Congress Cataloging in Publication Data

Race, William H.
    Pindar.

    (Twayne's world authors series; TWAS 773. Greek literature)
    Bibliography: p. 150
    Includes index.
    1. Pindar—Criticism and interpretation.
I. Pindar.   II. Title.
III. Series: Twayne's world authors series; TWAS 773.
IV. Series: Twayne's world authors series. Greek literature.
PA4276.R33   1986   884'.01   85-17576
ISBN 0-8057-6624-3

Contents

About the Author

William H. Race was graduated as a Phi Beta Kappa from the University of Michigan with a B.A. in Latin in 1965. After serving as a lieutenant in the army artillery, he received his Ph.D. in classics with a minor in comparative literature from Stanford University in 1973. He taught for three years at the University of California at Berkeley in classics and interdisciplinary studies, and is now an associate professor of classics at Vanderbilt University. Besides a monograph, *The Classical Priamel from Homer to Boethius,* he has published a dozen articles on aspects of Pindar, Plato, Isokrates, Horace, and Sappho.

Preface

There has been a great deal of interest in Pindar during recent years. Since 1969—in English alone—four complete translations of the odes have appeared, along with a half-dozen books and scores of articles in classical journals on various aspects of his poetry. And yet there is no general introduction to his works that can serve the needs of the general reader as well as classicists. The present study hopes to fill that need. It assumes no knowledge of Greek on the part of the reader, but yet intends to be of interest to those who can (on whatever level) follow the Greek text. It does not claim to make Pindar "easy"—for he is a very difficult poet—but it does aspire to make him more comprehensible and more accessible.

Although this study aims at a balanced account of Pindar's life, thought, and poetry, its emphasis is literary, and its primary purpose is to show what the odes of Pindar contain and how they are constructed. Thanks to the painstaking work of two generations of scholars—W. Schadewaldt, H. Gundert, S. L. Radt, L. Woodbury, E. L. Bundy, D. C. Young, and W. J. Slater (to name but a few)—we have gained a much greater understanding of the language, conventions, and themes operative in the odes. The present study is greatly indebted to their discoveries.

A word is in order about its limitations. Since the fragments of Pindar's other works are rarely translated and remain the concern of specialists, the study concentrates on the victory odes. Even then, limited space has made it impossible to treat all forty-five odes (some 3,400 verses). Consequently, there have been some regrettable omissions (e.g., *Ol.* 4, 5, 14; *Pyth.* 7, 10, 12; *Nem.* 2, 3, and 4). In addition, the bibliography is very selective. It does not duplicate references in the notes, and is intended as a survey of recent major work, mostly in English and easily available.

The translations are my own. They are not poetry; they are prose that follows as closely as possible the word order and verses of the original. Thus, the reader can get a good idea of the form and movement of the original, and can easily find the passage in a Greek text. I have, with some reluctance, adopted Greek spellings for all but the most familiar names (e.g., Athens, Thebes, Delphi, Corinth, Achilles,

Ajax, and Jason). There is, however, no longer any justification for filtering Greek names through Latin spellings. Furthermore, a number of translations (Lattimore, Bowra, and Nisetich) use Greek spellings and undoubtedly more will do so in the future. The reader may find *Sophokles* initially startling, but it is closer to his real name.

Finally, I wish to express my gratitude to the College of Arts and Science of Vanderbilt University for generously giving me a semester's leave to write the present work.

William H. Race

Vanderbilt University

Chronology

518 B.C.   Probable date for Pindar's birth at Kynoskephalai, a village adjacent to Thebes in the district of Boiotia.

498   Probable date of *Pyth.* 10, the earliest victory ode.

490   Battle of Marathon: Athenians defeat Persian expeditionary force sent by Darios.

480   Battle of Salamis: Athenians engineer this victory over the Persian fleet; the Aiginetan sailors win the prize for bravery. Battle of Himera: Gelon of Syracuse defeats Carthaginians.

479   Battle of Plataia: Spartans and allies defeat the Persian army.

476   Pindar writes five odes for Olympic victors in this year: *Ol.* 1 (Hieron of Syracuse), *Ol.* 2 and 3 (Theron of Akragas), and *Ol.* 10 and 11 (Hagesidamos of Western Lokroi).

476–475   Hieron founds city of Aitna.

474   Battle of Kyma (Cumae): Hieron defeats an Etruscan fleet.

470   Pindar writes *Pyth.* 1 to Hieron: Aischylos composes the *Aitnai*.

462   Pindar writes *Pyth.* 4 and 5 to Arkesilas of Kyrene.

446   Probable date of *Pyth.* 8, the last victory ode.

438   Probable date of Pindar's death.

Chapter One
Pindar's Life

The Basic Facts

We have surprisingly little accurate information about the life of Greece's greatest lyric poet. Although we possess five short accounts of his life from antiquity, they contain so many contradictory details that it is scarcely an exaggeration to say that there is only one fact on which all agree: Pindar was a Theban. Some even specify that he was born in Kynoskephalai, a village on the outskirts of Thebes.[1] Three candidates are given for his father, two for his mother, and three different ages at death: fifty-five, sixty-six, and eighty. The recently published papyrus from the late second or third century A.D. that contains a portion of a life of Pindar shows that even in antiquity there was confusion about the dates of his career.[2]

As a result, scholars must select the most probable information available to arrive at a likely chronology. His date of birth is uncertain, but scholars have generally accepted as true a fragment quoted from an unidentified poem to the effect that the poet was born during a Pythian festival.[3] Since Pythian festivals occurred during the third year of an Olympiad, the most likely years for his birth would be 522 or 518. Although either would be possible, recent scholarship has tended to favor the later date.

But the most important evidence for dating Pindar's career comes from the poems themselves, along with a papyrus written around 250 A.D. that records the Olympic victors for the years 480–468 and 456–448 B.C.[4] We thus have firm dates for most of the Olympian odes, ranging from 476 to 452 B.C. Furthermore, if we accept the dates given in the ancient commentaries, the earliest ode is *Pyth.* 10 in 498 and the latest is *Pyth.* 8 in 446.[5] Then, if the years 498–446 represent his active career, 518 would be a plausible date for his birth and 438 for his death (taking the eighty-year figure as the only one long enough).

Besides relating numerous anecdotes that will be treated below, the lives also tell us that Pindar studied fluteplaying with one Skopelinos (variously called his father or uncle), lyric composition with Lasos of Hermione, and music in Athens with Agathokles (or Apollodoros). His total production of choral lyric poetry was later collected into seventeen books of various types. Although numerous fragments of his paians (hymns to Apollo) and of other poems survive in papyri and through quotation by other ancient authors, only his four books of victory odes (epinikia) have been preserved almost intact, and it is with these that we will be principally concerned. Some of these odes are addressed to the most powerful men of the times, including the Sicilian tyrants Theron of Akragas and Hieron of Syracuse, and Arkesilas IV of Kyrene. Like his near contemporary Aischylos, it is probable that he was entertained in the court of Hieron, who was a great patron of the arts. His odes are for victors all over Greece, and their geographical range is very impressive: the Sicilian cities of Syracuse, Akragas, Himera, and Kamarina, Western Lokroi in Italy, Kyrene (in modern Libya), Thessaly, Athens, Argos, Corinth, Rhodes, Tenedos, Aigina, and, of course, Thebes. We cannot be certain from his poems whether he was present at the performances, nor do we know what contractual arrangements were made ahead of time. But it can be assumed that he traveled widely during his life, and perhaps directed some of the choruses that sang his songs. One date does, however, stand out in his career, the Olympic year of 476, which occasioned the writing of five odes: *Ol.* 1 for Hieron's victory in the horse race, *Ol.* 2 and 3 for Theron's victory in the chariot race, and *Ol.* 10 and 11 for Hagesidamos of Western Lokroi, who won the boys' boxing match. Such is the bare outline of Pindar's career.[6]

The Anecdotes

The lives of Pindar contain a number of anecdotes that have little or no historical value. But since they form a part of the ancient tradition surrounding the poet, and serve to illustrate important aspects of his career and art, they have a certain exemplary value, and are worth retelling.

One story relates that when Pindar was a boy, he was hunting near Mt. Helikon, and fell asleep from exhaustion. A bee then built a honeycomb in his mouth.[7] The author of the life in which this account is found cites Chamaileon as an authority for it. Since Chamaileon was a biographer of the early third century B.C., we can assume that these tales were current within a century or more of the poet's death. It is, of course, a familiar folktale motif meant to indicate the precocious literary genius of the poet (the same story is told, for example, of Plato). But particularly important is the geographical detail, for it was while shepherding his sheep under Mt. Helikon (the highest mountain in Boiotia, about twenty miles from Thebes), that Pindar's fellow Boiotian poet Hesiod (ca. 750 B.C.) received his poetic calling from the Muses.[8] Mt. Helikon had become famous as a haunt of the Muses, and the anecdote attempts to link the two greatest poets from Boiotia. The choice of the bee is also appropriate, because Pindar uses the image of a bee to describe his poetry (*Pyth.* 10.53–54), and is fond of calling his songs "honey-voiced" or "honey-sounding."

Another anecdote about his early career links him with Korinna, a Boiotian poetess.[9] She supposedly criticized the aspiring poet for priding himself on his stylistic embellishments rather than on telling myths. Thereupon, he composed a poem which begins: "Shall we sing of Ismenos, or of Melia with the golden distaff, or of Kadmos . . ." and continues with five more possibilities. When she heard this, Korinna laughed and said, "One should sow with the hand, not the whole sack." The lines in question are in fact the beginning verses of the great "Hymn to Zeus" that opened the collection of Pindar's hymns.[10] The story is a humorous illustration of Pindar's exuberant use of mythical catalogs to introduce his poems[11] and of his generous references to myths and legends throughout his works.

Another story, with surer historical basis, gained considerable currency in antiquity. Soon after the Persian war (see "Historical Background," below), he began a famous dithyramb with high praise of Athens' conduct during the war with the words: "O gleaming, violet-crowned, illustrious in song, bulwark of Hellas, famous Athens, divine citadel" (fr. 76). One version, among many,[12] states that the Thebans fined him 1,000 drachmas for praising their enemy, but the Athenians paid the fine for him out of gratitude. The anecdote attempts to explain why a Theban poet, whose native city fought on the Persian side during the war, would praise Athens for its victory. At issue here is the tension between Pindar the Theban and Pindar the Panhellenic poet. Although he was subject to the intense rivalries among the cities he celebrated, he rose above mere partisanship, and consistently gave praise where it was fairly earned. Then, too, the story illustrates another point: poetry was taken seriously and was worth a great deal of money.

A number of anecdotes mention Pindar's close relationship to the gods. We are told that someone once heard the god Pan singing a paian of his between Mt. Kithairon and Mt. Helikon (both in Boiotia). Also, Demeter supposedly blamed him in a dream for neglecting her in his poems, whereupon he composed a hymn in her honor. It is also reported that the priest at Apollo's temple at Delphi announced at closing each day, "Let Pindar join the gods at dinner." The second-century A.D. traveler Pausanias reports that he was shown the iron chair at Delphi where Pindar supposedly composed his paians.[13] All these tales reflect the deeply religious nature of his poetry, and in particular his great devotion to Apollo, for whom he wrote many hymns and who figures very prominently in the victory odes.

And finally, there is the famous story of Pindar's house, which Alexander the Great supposedly spared when he razed Thebes in 335 B.C.[14] Milton's lines in sonnet 8 have made the event well known to English readers: "The great Emathian conquerer bid spare / The house of Pindarus, when temple and tow'r / Went to the ground." Although some have rightly doubted the historical validity of the story,[15] it serves to illustrate the international reputation that Pindar had gained in the century following his death. It is also fitting that the commander who was uniting all Greece against the Persians and who venerated Homer would appreciate the Panhellenic poet who celebrated the deeds of great men.

Historical Background

The years from 500 to 440 B.C.—approximately the period of Pindar's active career—were among the most eventful in Greek history. These years were preceded by the flowering of the scores of city states called *poleis* (singular, *polis*), and the great expansion of Greek culture in settlements along the Mediterranean coast from Marseilles to southern Italy, Sicily, Libya, and to the shores of the Black Sea. And some of these cities, like Syracuse, Akragas, and Kyrene, rivaled the mainland Greek cities in power and wealth.

But Greece was not the only culture expanding its horizons during this period. Between 550 and 500 the Persian Empire came to dominate the entire Middle East from Egypt to India, and was threatening to engulf Greece as well. In 490 Darios, the king of Persia, sent an expeditionary force to punish Athens for aiding an earlier Ionian revolt. Supported only by a contingent from the little city of Plataia, the Athenians defeated the Persians on the plain of Marathon about thirty miles from Athens. This victory gave Athens a great boost toward leadership among the Greek cities and inspired her future resistance to the Persian threat. Although the imminent invasion of Greece was delayed by the death of Darios in 486, his successor Xerxes launched a full-scale attack by land and sea in 480. This vast army and navy appeared invincible, and in spite of a valiant holding effort at the pass of Thermopylai, it seemed but a matter of time before all Greece would fall. The northern cities, notably Thebes, threw in with the invaders. But the Athenians took to their ships and left their city to be destroyed by the Persians. Then, in two decisive battles, the Greeks soundly defeated the invaders. The Athenians, who had the largest fleet of the Greeks, engineered the sea battle of Salamis in 480 and with the combined Greek forces effectively crippled the Persian fleet. Although the Athenians took credit for the overall battle, the ships from the island of Aigina were most conspicuous for their bravery during the fighting. Then, after wintering in Thessaly, the Persians met the Greeks the following year (479) in a decisive land battle at Plataia, located between Thebes and Athens. Oddly enough, the Thebans fought against the Athenians and actually defeated them, but the Spartans managed to rout the Persians and killed their commander Mardonios. The Persian threat was over, but this hour of glory for Greece was a shameful one for Thebes, which remained a bitter enemy of Athens for the next century. We have no idea how Pindar the Theban took this disgrace personally, but in his poems he consistently praises Athens, Sparta, and Aigina for freeing Greece from that "rock of Tantalos."[16]

And while the Persians were invading from the east, the Carthaginians were attacking Sicily from the west. In 480 a coalition of Sicilian Greeks under the leadership of Gelon of Syracuse (Hieron's older brother) and Theron of Akragas crushed a large Carthaginian army at Himera on the north coast of the island. Tradition places this battle on the same day as the Battle of Salamis. Then in 474 Hieron defeated an Etruscan fleet off Kyma (Cumae) near the Bay of Naples, thereby averting a threat to the Greeks in southern Italy.[17] Pindar celebrated these victories in *Pyth.* 1, which will be examined in detail later.

After the defeat of the Persians in 479, Athens steadily came to dominate Greek affairs, both politically and culturally. She controlled the seas with her navy and headed a confederacy of maritime states throughout the Aegean that gradually became a tributary "empire." Along with this power and wealth came a cultural revolution that included the development of tragedy, radical experiments in democracy, and important contributions to philosophy and architecture. Under the guidance of Perikles from 461 until his death in 429, Athens made a bid to become the cultural center of all Greece, the "School of Hellas," as Perikles is reported to have boasted in his "Funeral Oration."[18] During the last four decades of Pindar's career, the Athenian dramatists Aischylos and Sophokles were perfecting tragedy, work was begun on the Parthenon (447), and Anaxagoras and Protagoras were initiating a philosophical revolution that would culminate in the Athenian genius, Sokrates.

But this burst of Athenian energy also produced a strong resistance, and tended to split the Greek world into two opposing camps. Put broadly, the one side was represented by Athenian democracy, innovation, aggressive economic imperialism, and radically new philosophical ideas, while the other centered around Spartan aristocratic institutions based on Doric traditions, conservatism, defensive foreign policy, and traditional ideas. The split eventually led to the disastrous Peloponnesian War (431–404) that ended in Athenian defeat. In his history of that war, the Athenian historian Thukydides neatly sums up the differences between the two sides in a speech of the Corinthians warning the Spartans about Athenian character:

An Athenian is always an innovator, quick to form a resolution and quick at carrying it out. You, on the other hand, are good at keeping things as they are; you never originate an idea, and your action tends to stop short of its aim. . . . Think of this, too: while you are hanging back, they never hesitate; while you stay at home, they are always abroad . . . . Of them alone it may be said that they possess a thing almost as soon as they have begun to desire it, so quickly with them does action follow upon decision. And so they go on working away in hardship and danger all the days of their lives, seldom enjoying their possessions because they are always adding to them. Their view of a holiday is to do what needs doing; they prefer hardship and activity to peace and quiet. In a word, they are by nature incapable of either living a quiet life themselves or of allowing anyone else to do so.[19]

There is no doubt on which side Pindar's natural sympathies fall. He regularly praises aristocrats, Doric laws and institutions, and political stability; his view looks back to the traditional legends and wisdom; he is wary of what is not tried and true. But it must be emphasized that Pindar was no ideologue. He praises Athens in glowing terms whenever he mentions her and writes two odes (*Pyth.* 7 and *Nem.* 2) for Athenians. Surprisingly, there are no odes to any Spartan victors. The splendid achievements of Athens are beyond dispute, but their brilliance has tended to blind us to the beauties of other aspects of Greek life. Pindar is important for providing that other perspective. And while his art soars in inimitable language, his thought is on the whole cautionary. It is full of warnings about man's dependence upon the gods, his limitations, and the hardships of life. His message, if there is one, is essentially that of the mottoes on Apollo's temple at Delphi: "Know Thyself" and "Nothing in Excess."

Chapter Two

The Works of Pindar

History of the Text

The works of Pindar were first collected and edited at the royal library at Alexandria in Egypt, founded by the Ptolemies shortly after 300 B.C. The most important early editor was Aristophanes of Byzantium, head librarian from about 194 to 180 B.C. He arranged the works into seventeen "books" (papyrus rolls) comprising *hymnoi* to various gods (1 book); *paianes*, special hymns addressed to Apollo (1); *dithyramboi*, special hymns addressed to Dionysos (2); *prosodia*, hymns for approaching a god's shrine (2); *partheneia*, hymns sung by maidens (3); *hyporchēmata*, dancing hymns (2); *enkōmia*, lighter songs of praise for men at banquets (1); *thrēnoi*, songs of lament for men (1); and *epinikia*, victory songs (4).[1]

Later editors, notably Aristarchos of Samothrace (ca. 217–145 B.C.) and Didymos (ca. 80–10 B.C.), added lengthy commentaries to the text. Bits and pieces of these have come down to us as marginal notes (scholia) in our manuscripts. In the third century A.D. the other books of Pindar's poems began to drop out of circulation and only the four books of epinicians continued to be read.[2] It was probably during this time that the papyrus rolls were transfered to book form (*codex*), and not long afterward two distinct families of manuscripts took shape. These families are known as the "Ambrosian recension," named for the most important representative, a thirteenth-century manuscript in the Ambrosian Library in Milan, and the "Vatican recension," named for a twelfth-century manuscript in the Vatican Library. In addition, there are numerous manuscripts deriving from editions by Byzantine scholars in the thirteenth and fourteenth centuries A.D. There are, altogether, more than 180 manuscripts of all or part of Pindar's epinikia.

Until the turn of the century we only possessed "fragments" from Pindar's other books, consisting of words or a few lines quoted by ancient authors to illustrate some point that generally had nothing to do with the original intention of the poet. But in 1906 the English scholars Grenfell and Hunt published considerable remains of the *pai-anes* found in the papyrus rubbish heap at Oxyrhynchus in Egypt.[3] These papyrus fragments antedate our earliest manuscripts by many centuries. On the whole, this additional material has broadened our understanding of Pindar, but it has not significantly altered what we already knew from the epinicians. All of his works demonstrate a remarkable consistency of style and language.[4]

The victory odes. When the Alexandrian editors faced the task of organizing the Pindaric corpus into coherent groups of lengths suitable for papyrus rolls, there were so many victory odes that they adopted the expedient of grouping them according to the four major games: the Olympian, Pythian, Isthmian, and Nemean, in their order of relative antiquity and prestige. Then, within each "book" the odes were classified by event, beginning with the equestrian (*hippika*) events (in order of chariot race, horse race, and mule cart race) and continuing with the "gymnastic" (*gymnastika*) events (in order of pankration, wrestling, boxing, pentathlon, and foot races). The last Pythian ode (12) even celebrates a victory in flute playing.

Since only the wealthy could afford to maintain and transport race horses of the caliber to win at the great games, this arrangement tended to give pride of place in each book of odes to the greatest patrons. The first editors undoubtedly intended to make the introductory poems in each collection as striking as possible. The position of the first *Olympian* ode is an interesting case in point. Although Theron's victory in the chariot race would normally take precedence, the two odes celebrating the event (*Ol.* 2 and 3) follow *Ol.* 1, which celebrates Hieron's victory in the single horse race. We are told that Aristophanes of Byzantium placed this ode first in the collection because it contained praise of the Olympic games and told of Pelops, the first to compete at Elis, the future location of the games.[5]

There are some other interesting anomalies in the collection. For example, it is questionable whether *Pyth.* 2 celebrates a Pythian victory and *Pyth.* 3 apparently refers to past victories. But since they do mention athletic victories (although rather vaguely), they were included among the epinikia and placed after *Pyth.* 1, which clearly celebrates Hieron's Pythian chariot victory, presumably to form a group of odes to Pindar's greatest patron. These then came ahead of *Pyth.* 4 and 5 for Arkesilas's chariot victory. The last three odes in the Nemean collection are even more anomalous: *Nem.* 9 for a chariot victory in the Sikyonian games, *Nem.* 10 for a wrestling victory in Argive games, and *Nem.* 11 on the occasion of a former athlete's installation as a magistrate on the island of Tenedos. It is apparent that the few odes that would not fit the four-game classification were added at the end of the Nemean odes, also in order of event: equestrian, gymnastic, other. These Nemean odes originally must have been at the end of the collection, but at some point, probably when the papyrus rolls were copied into one codex, the Nemean and Isthmian books were reversed. In time, some of the final pages of the last book were destroyed, and as a result the end of the Isthmian book is fragmentary. We have a few lines of a ninth Isthmian and some indication that there were yet others. But the collection is, with that exception, complete.

In the transmission of works of literature from antiquity, with repeated copying by hand, mistakes inevitably accrue in the manuscripts. But the text of the epinicians is remarkably sound—far more so than that, say, of Aischylos. Thanks to the labors of ancient, Renaissance, and modern editors, there is general agreement on most of the readings, and there are only a couple dozen or so small places where a word or at most a sentence is in real doubt. The soundness of the text is both important and surprising in view of the great difficulty of Pindar's language, and although hundreds of emendations have been proposed,[6] the variations among texts of this century are slight. There are no gaps or lacunae in the text, and with only one questionable case,[7] the integrity of each poem is guaranteed.

The scholia.   The manuscripts of the epinikia preserve extensive commentary in the margins. These annotations, scholia (singular, scholium), represent a sifting process during the centuries before the formation of the two major recensions of the text. As a result, the scholia of the Ambrosian recension differ from those of the Vatican.[8] Many of the scholia derive from the commentary of Didymos compiled in the Augustan period (ca. 20 B.C.), and some even preserve comments of the earliest Alexandrian editors such as Aristarchos. Their quality is very uneven; sometimes they merely paraphrase the text, sometimes they are simply fanciful. Although dozens of interesting examples could be given, one will have to suffice. Pindar begins *Pyth.* 1 to his greatest patron, Hieron of Syracuse, with a hymn to the lyre, beginning "Golden Lyre." Here is the introductory comment: "According to Artemon the historian, Pindar begins in this manner because Hieron had promised him a golden cithara. But such explanations are superfluous, for it is entirely appropriate for him to hymn the god who presides over the Pythian festival."[9] In this case, an anonymous scholiast records an earlier conjecture in order to refute it. The two views illustrate two different ways of approaching the text: the one looks for an "historical" explanation outside the work, the other looks for an explanation based on the "genre" of the poem. These two trends run throughout the scholia and modern criticism as well. Often there are two or more scholia on a passage, sometimes offering radically different interpretations.

All in all, the scholia are not only of great assistance for interpreting the text, but they also provide an engaging record of the history of ancient scholarship. The scholiasts wrestled with the same problems we do today: variant readings, historical allusions, difficulties of grammar, dialect, and meter, complications of dating, rhetorical and poetic anomalies, logical coherence, mythological references, and translation into plain prose. In fact, almost all modern controversies, whether concerned with overall approaches or with specific passages, find their counterpart in the ancient scholia.

One would naturally suppose that those commentators who were writing within a few centuries of Pindar would have had a complete command of his language, poetry, and historical background, or at least would have understood his work much better than we do at a remove of twenty-five centuries. This is not necessarily so. Pindar's works reflect the worldview of the "archaic" period (ca. 650–480 B.C.), whereas the scholia derive from the "Hellenistic" (ca. 300–150 B.C.) and later periods. The shift in language and thought that occurred between these two periods was so great that Pindar's poetry had already become strange if not often incomprehensible. A modern analogy might be the similar shift between the Renaissance period and the Enlightenment, as evidenced, for example, by Voltaire's disdain of Shakespeare, whose plays offended his sense of logic and decorum. The trend in the twentieth century has been toward a greater appreciation of archaic poetry and art, and as a result, recent scholarship has tried to put aside controversies that arise from Hellenistic preoccupations and to understand Pindar on his own terms. More than any other, the work of E. L. Bundy has pointed the way toward a better understanding of the language, rhetoric, and conventions of the epinician genre.[10]

Pindar's Poetry

Meter and form. The meters of Greek choral lyric poetry are very complex and a full discussion is beyond the scope of this book. The basic metrical principles and form of the odes are, however, quite easy to grasp. A glance at the Greek text immediately shows that groups of uneven lines are printed in blocks or stanzas. The first stanza, consisting of anywhere from three to thirteen lines, is called a "strophe." Seven odes (*Ol.* 14; *Pyth.* 6, 12; *Nem.* 2, 4, 9; and *Isth.* 8) repeat the metrical pattern of this strophe two to twelve times. These odes are called "monostrophic." The thirty-eight remaining odes are "triadic," in which the initial strophe is followed by another metrically identical stanza called an "antistrophe," and this in turn is followed by a different stanza called an "epode." Five odes (*Ol.* 4, 11, 12; *Pyth.* 7; and *Isth.* 3) consist of only one triad. The remainder contain from three to thirteen triads, each metrically identical, so that all the strophes and antistrophes within a poem correspond to one another, as do all the epodes.

The strophe itself consists of "long" and "short" syllables that constitute a rhythmic pattern. There are rules for determining whether a syllable is long or short,[11] but for our purposes the important thing to note is that Greek meter is "quantitative," that is, a long syllable is held longer than a short, on the analogy of a quarter note and an eighth note. There is, then, a close relationship between Greek meter and music. English, on the other hand, is "qualitative," for its rhythm is determined by the stress, not length, of syllables, and its scansion consists of "heavy" and "light" syllables. Greek has no appreciable stress, and the accents printed in the texts represent pitch. Thus Tennyson's playful line of dactylic hexameter, "Jack was a poor widow's heir, but he lived as a drone in a beehive," is scanned ′ u u ′ u u ′ u u ′ u u ′ u u ′ ′ because it consists of a series of stressed and unstressed syllables. The first line of the *Odyssey* (also dactylic hexameter), "andra moi ennepe, Mousa, polytropon hos mala polla," is scanned — u u — u u — u u — u u — u u — — because the longs are held twice as long as the shorts.

The poet has considerable freedom in creating the first strophe of an ode. With one exception (*Isth.* 3 and 4) Pindar never duplicates the form of a strophe from one ode to another; each is a unique creation, consisting of different patterns of longs and shorts. But once the poet creates one strophe, he must repeat the same metrical pattern (with different words, of course) in an answering antistrophe. Thus the original freedom is followed by the constraint of exact repetition. Then, if the poem continues beyond one triad, each successive triad must be identical. While most odes have three to five triads, the remarkable *Pyth.* 4 has thirteen triads and is 299 lines long.

The poet is not entirely free to create random rhythms. Most odes fall into two general categories of rhythms, called dactylo-epitritic and Aeolic. The former combines the basic metra of dactyls (— u u), especially in larger units called "hemiepes" (— u u — u u —), and epitrites (— u — —). It is a stately rhythm and Pindar refers to it as "Doric." The Aeolic rhythm is much freer and is composed mainly of iambs (u —) and choriambs (— u u —). The odes are roughly half in each rhythm. One—*Ol.* 13—combines the two, with strophes and antistrophes in Aeolic and the epodes in dactylo-epitritic, while *Ol.* 2 is the only epinician with a meter based on iambs and cretics (— u —).

Overall, the structure of Pindar's odes conveys the impression of great variety, creativity, and virtuosity. The form leaves room for daring experimentation and yet demands exacting discipline. There is a constant tension between freedom and restraint. For example, Pindar opens *Ol.* 13 with a striking seven-syllable compound adjective, *trisolympionikan* (u u — u u — —), "thrice-olympic-victorious." The one-word verse is tailor-made for the occasion, and yet he must repeat the same rhythm nine more times in successive strophes and antistrophes.

Performance. We know very little about the actual performances of these odes. Like the choral odes of Attic tragedy to which they are closely related, they were probably sung by a choir that also danced in accompaniment to lyres and wind instruments. We do not know if they were always danced, or how the dancers moved. Late sources say that the chorus danced the strophe with movements in one direction, while they reversed direction for the antistrophe and stood still for the epode.[12] Indeed, the word strophe means "turn," but epode simply means "after-song."[13] Many commentators assume that the monostrophic odes were processional. But all of this is highly speculative. By the time the scholia were written, any clear notion of the original music or dance seems to have been lost.

There are many references in the odes to their performance by choirs (sometimes specified as "boys" or companions of the victor), to the accompanying instruments, and even to the choir director. Such remarks, however, give only a vague indication of what the performance would have been like. We know from the analogy of Attic drama that the outfitting and training of a chorus were a laborious and expensive enterprise. Presumably the grand odes were performed in lavish splendor with highly trained choruses; maybe others were performed by hometown groups. We do not know when Pindar may have been present, or whether he might have helped train the choir. He often talks of his presence with such remarks as "I have come," "I stand here," but it is often difficult to be certain if this is the actual "I" of the poet or a conventional persona. Indeed, in some odes there is a contradictory reference to the poet "being present" and yet "sending" his praises.[14]

It would, of course, be very interesting to know more about the music and dance of Pindar's odes, but this loss is not as critical as some would have us believe. Indeed, tragedy presents an analogous case. In his *Poetics*, chapter 6, Aristotle observes that music and spectacle are the least important components of tragedy, and although they give pleasure, they are dispensable. "Of the other elements which 'enrich' tragedy the most important is song-making. Spectacle, while highly effective, is yet quite foreign to the art and has nothing to do with poetry. Indeed the effect of tragedy does not depend on its performance by actors, and, moreover, for achieving the spectacular effects the art of the costumier is more authoritative than that of the poet."[15] If one substitutes "dancers" for "actors," the passage could well apply to Pindar. Like the tragedians Aischylos, Sophokles, and Euripides, Pindar clearly composed his odes for posterity—not to be performed once and forgotten—and the essential effect of his odes exists independently of any performance. We have the text of the odes, and that is probably all we shall ever have. The loss of music and choreography is more of a loss for the history of those arts than an insurmountable barrier to the understanding of Pindar's poetry, whose odes were clearly written to be read again and again. For that very reason they survived their original performance.

Language.   Nothing is more dazzling (or perhaps more difficult) in a Pindaric ode than the language. First of all, it is a literary language, not a spoken one. It is an artificial creation of generations of poets, and although it contains many elements from other dialects, Doric forms predominate.[16] This Doric coloring was a regular feature of the genre of choral lyric, and when an Athenian playwright composed the lyric passages of his plays, instead of his own Attic dialect he used some Doric elements. Pindar's contemporary Bacchylides of Keos was an Ionian; nevertheless, his choral odes contain Doric forms.

The student who first encounters Pindar in Greek, and who spends a half-hour trying to make sense of a seven-word sentence, who consults dictionaries, commentaries, and translations and still remains baffled, cannot help but wonder how the original listeners could have understood what was being said. But the same is said of the audiences of Greek tragedy and of Shakespeare and applies to all great literary artists, whose works deepen with each successive hearing or reading. There can be no doubt about it: Pindar must have been difficult for his own audience. He certainly became so for commentators in the next two centuries. But the Greeks had a common saying: "chalepa ta kala," (beautiful things are difficult). Surely the original audience was used to the extreme compression and contortion of language and knew the conventions of the genre, so that they could follow a Pindaric ode, although much would become clearer on subsequent readings. Likewise, the student of Pindar gradually becomes accustomed to the style and finds the language more and more familiar—and enjoyable.

Word order.   Greek, like Latin, is an inflected language, and since the terminations of words indicate the word's use in the sentence (rather than word order as in English), the poet can achieve amazing feats of syntactical skill. For example, at *Ol.* 12.5–6, Pindar puts thirteen words between an article and its noun. The flexibility of Greek also permits complex interlocking word order.[17] A literal translation of Pindaric Greek demonstrates this point: "ōpase de Kroniōn polemou mnastēra hoi chalkenteos laon hippaichmon" (*Nem.* 1.16–17) translates directly into English as "gave and Kronos's son of war enamored to her bronze-armored people of armed horsemen." From this one can see the justice in Abraham Cowley's famous remark in the opening of the preface to his Pindarique odes (1656): "If a man should undertake to translate Pindar word for word, it would be thought that one mad-man had translated another." Yet out of this interlocking puzzle comes: "And Kronos's son (Zeus) gave to her (Sicily) a people of armed horsemen enamored of bronze-armored war." In the preceding lines, Pindar had been praising Sicily for her rich agriculture and wealthy cities, and here he turns to her people. The word order allows him to hold back the crucial word *laon* (people) and emphasize it by placing it first in the next line ("enjambment"). Finally, he ends with the modifier *hippaichmon* (of armed horsemen). The compound takes on special importance, since this is an ode to a Sicilian who has won the chariot race at Nemea. It also leads naturally into the following mention (17–18) of Sicilian success at the Olympic games. More could be said about the artful balance of these verses. Suffice it to say that Pindar is a master of parallel and chiastic (criss-cross) interlocking of words, and the careful reader is continually surprised by the remarkable variety and subtlety of Pindar's word order.

Compound adjectives.   Pindar also takes advantage of another resource of the Greek language: the creation of compound words. In the line from *Nem.* 1.16–17 quoted above, the word *hippaichmon* (of armed horsemen) may well have been invented for this very ode, since the word appears nowhere else in extant Greek writings. The other compound *chalkenteos* (bronze-armored) only appears one other place, and it is also in Pindar (at *Nem.* 11.35). Indeed, compound words, especially adjectives, are a regular feature of choral lyric, and there are scores of them in the odes. For example, there are seven in the first triad of *Nem.* 1 including the two just mentioned. The frequent use of compounds is a component of what came to be known as the "grand style," and if allowances are not made, they may appear bombastic or merely ornamental. Pindar's verse is remarkably free of these two faults: his compounds almost always indicate careful consideration and add significantly to the meaning, sound, or imagery.[18]

Metaphors. Another aspect of Pindaric language is delight in metaphor. For example, in the lines quoted above from *Nem.* 1, *mnastēra* (enamored) literally means "wooer," and is the term applied to the suitors of Penelope in the *Odyssey.* The metaphor indicates the eagerness with which the Sicilians engage in war (and also athletics). Moderns are warned against "mixed metaphors," but Pindar enjoys them as part of his rich and varied language. For example, at *Isth.* 1.64–65 he describes the victor as "lifted up on the bright wings of the tuneful Pierian Maidens."[19] This phrase contains three important categories from which Pindar constantly draws metaphors to describe victory and its celebration. "Lifted up" and "wings" indicate height; "bright" (boldly describing wings) connotes light and splendor; "tuneful" adds the dimension of sound. Pindar is fond of combining words associated with height and distance ("flying," "soaring," "exalted," "far and wide"), brightness ("light," "brilliance," "shining," "blazing," "radiant"), and sound ("song," "fame," "voice," "sing out," "shout," "celebrate").[20] To take but one example, fame can "bloom" or "wither," "gleam" or "fall asleep"; it can be "deep," "wide," "high," or "big"; it can "fly," "shine," or even "look out into the distance."

One of the largest groups of metaphorical expressions clusters around the activity of writing poetry. In order to describe his poetic art, Pindar draws concepts and terms from such activities as plowing, sailing, chariot driving, archery, wrestling, architecture, sculpture, weaving, javelin throwing, and business. Song can be a "crown," a "mirror," a "building," a "storehouse," a "drink," a "toast," a "healing remedy," or "charm."[21]

Of the hundreds of metaphors, some are so subtle as scarcely to be noticed, while others are very memorable. Two, for example, concern food and fittingly occur in an ode full of "eating," *Ol.* 1, where Tantalos could not "digest" (55) his great prosperity, while Pelops contrasts the life of heroic action with one who "boils" or "stews" (83) a nameless old age while sitting in darkness. At *Pyth.* 4.186, in a similar vein, Pindar describes the stay-at-home as "nursing" a life without danger beside his mother. And perhaps his most powerful metaphor describes the insubstantiality of human existence at *Pyth.* 8.95–96: *skias onar / anthrōpos,* literally, "(of a) shadow (the) dream / mankind": "man is the dream of a shadow."

Negative expressions. Another prominent feature of his style is the use of negative expressions to present positive ideas, thus giving depth and variety to the poetry.[22] By denying a negative quality, for example "not inexperienced in beautiful things" (*Ol.* 11.18), the positive is asserted in a kind of understatement ("litotes") with considerable delicacy and subtlety of effect. To take but one example out of dozens, at the end of *Isth.* 8, the boy victor is praiseworthy "because he did not repress in a hole a youth without experience of beautiful things." This sentence, a bit more awkward in translation than in the original, is an elaborate way of saying "the young man achieved glory." But by casting it in the negative, Pindar reminds us of what might have been the case (and all too often is): one's youth is prevented from developing its powers to the fullest extent; it is a youth that never comes to experience "beautiful things," that remains "in a hole." In this way, Pindar paints a dark background of unrealized potential, so that we can better appreciate the importance of the boy's success.

Similes. Pindar uses a number of brief similes throughout his poems. For example, at *Ol.* 2.86–88, inferior poets who are merely learners are "like a pair of crows that vainly cry against the divine bird of Zeus [the eagle]." At *Pyth.* 2.80 the poet is "like a cork above the waves, " while at *Ol.* 1.1–2, gold shines "like fire at night." On three occasions he uses elaborate similes to characterize his poetic task: *Ol.* 7.1–10, where he compares his poetry of celebration to the toast of wine at a wedding; *Ol.* 10.86–90, where he compares his late ode to an heir finally come to an aging man; and *Isth.* 6.1–9, where he compares his poems to the three "toasts" at a drinking party. Very often, however, Pindar will omit the word "like" and simply appear in the guise of an archer (*Ol.* 2.83, 9.5), or javelin thrower (*Ol.* 13.93), or ship captain (*Nem.* 4.69–70, 5.50–51).

Sound and imagery. Although the sound of Pindar's language is rich and full,[23] he is much more sparing than, say, Aischylos or Lucretius in the use of alliteration, and the one place where he clearly intends it is famous. In *Pyth*. 1, he concludes his description of the eruption of Mt. Aitna with: "but at night the tumbling red flame carries boulders into the deep expanse of the sea with a crash." The final words in Greek are "pherei pontou plaka syn patagōi," where the repeated *p*'s imitate the sound of the crashing rocks.

It is clear that Pindar delights in playing with language. He often echoes words over and over in an ode, or draws on vocabulary that is conceptually interrelated, or even appears to be sensitive to "imagery."[24] So frequent and pronounced are these verbal echoes that in the nineteenth century F. Mezger cataloged most of them and argued that they provided the key for understanding Pindar.[25] Many scholars have paid careful attention to these verbal repetitions,[26] but while they constitute a fascinating aspect of Pindar's art, interpreters are often inclined to give them undue importance for understanding the poem, and sometimes end up with ingenious, but implausible, interpretations.

Wordplay. Pindar also enjoys wordplay and occasional puns. More obvious examples include the association of *ion* (violet) with the man's name *Iamos* in *Ol*. 6.55, *aietos* (eagle) with the name *Aias* at *Isth*. 6.53, and perhaps *ath*lete with *Ath*ens at *Nem*. 5.49. There are numerous others, but as in the case of "echoes," they are more an expression of exuberant use of language and ornamentation than serious indicators of meaning.

All in all, Pindar's language is extraordinarily complex, abundant, and difficult. The beginner is initially overwhelmed; but slowly the confusion gives way to appreciation and admiration. There is nothing quite like Pindar's language; at times it is lush to the point of cloying, at others so succinct that it is obscure; at times it is grandiose, at others plain, if not homely; it is always full of variety and surprises. It is, as Horace said, inimitable.[27]

Chapter Three

The Victory Odes

Greek Athletics

Athletics held a central position in Greek life and had religious, political, social, and even ethnic significance. So important were the Olympic games that their founding date of 776 B.C. marked the beginning of historical time for the Greeks. One common method of dating an event was to say that it occurred during one of the years of a particular Olympiad. Modern historians also use 776 B.C. as a convenient marker for the transition from the so-called "dark age" of Greece to the "archaic" period, as if the games somehow constituted a "light." Pindar would have appreciated such an image.[1]

The major festivals. The Olympic games were held in the northwestern part of the Peloponnesos in the district of Elis. They were followed by the institution of the Pythian and Isthmian games (ca. 582) and the Nemean games (ca. 573). Although there were dozens of local games by Pindar's time, some of which offered very lucrative prizes, these four games retained their status as the "holy," "Panhellenic," or "crown" games, at which the symbol of victory was a crown of wild olive at Olympia, laurel at Delphi, pine or dry parsley at the Isthmos, and green parsley at Nemea. An athlete who won in all four major games was called a *periodonikēs* (circuit-victor).

The Olympian and Pythian games were held every four years, with the Pythian occurring during the third year of an Olympiad. The Isthmian and Nemean games were held, alternately, every two years. Thus the four years during the 76th Olympiad (476–472 B.C.) would have had the following schedule: (1) 476: August, Olympic games; (2) 475: July, Nemean games; (3) 474: April, Isthmian games; August, Pythian games; (4) 473: July, Nemean games; 472: April, Isthmian games; August, 77th Olympiad begins. This constant sequence of games gave an opportunity for a talented athlete to compile an impressive catalog of victories. And the major games were just the top of the iceberg. As an example, the famed boxer, Diagoras of Rhodes, celebrated in *Ol.* 7 (464 B.C.), was a *periodonikēs* who had won once at Olympia, once at

Delphi, four times at the Isthmos, numerous times at Nemea and Athens, six times at Aigina and Megara, along with victories in games at Argos, Arcadia, Thebes, Boiotia, Pellana, and Rhodes.

The Olympic games always remained "the greatest of contests"[2] and served as a focal point for Hellenic interests. During the time of the games, heralds proclaimed a truce throughout Greece granting immunity to all who wished to travel to the games; and all Greeks by birth, regardless of their city, were eligible to compete—if they met the stringent training requirements for participating.[3] The five-day festival honored Zeus in particular, but there were altars for all the Olympian gods in the sanctuary. Local patriotism undoubtedly ran high as city vied with rival city for prominence in the displays of wealth and in the contests themselves, but the festival was truly Panhellenic, and was supervised by the impartial city of Elis under the strictest of regulations. This festival, more than any other event, united the Greeks as an ethnic community, in spite of bitter division among individual *poleis*.

The Pythian games at Delphi enjoyed much the same Panhellenic prestige. Apollo's famous oracle was there, and for two centuries it had played an important part in the religion and politics of Greece. The sanctuary was governed by a council comprised of representatives from numerous cities and thus maintained its independence as a spokesman for all Greece. Since Apollo was the god of music, there were originally musical competitions as well as gymnastic, and *Pyth.* 12 celebrates the victory of Midas of Akragas in flute playing.

The Isthmian games were held at Corinth on the Isthmos between the Peloponnesos and the mainland in honor of Poseidon, god of the sea. Corinth was a wealthy maritime city, conveniently located and noted for its lavish festivals. The Nemean games in honor of Zeus were located near the city of Kleonai, between Corinth and Argos. Until 460 they were supervised by Kleonai, afterward by Argos. Thus, with the exception of Delphi, which lies on the mainland, the other major games were located in the northern part of the Peloponnesos.

The athletic events.   In spite of some minor variations, the athletic programs at the four major games were very similar and included equestrian and "gymnastic" (i.e., nonequestrian) events. Some of the latter also had separate divisions for boys (whose ages probably ranged from twelve to eighteen years). During Pindar's time the equestrian events at Olympia consisted of the four horse chariot race, single horse race, and mule cart race; the gymnastic events were the *pankration* (all-strength) (a combination of wrestling and boxing), wrestling, boxing, the *pentathlon* (five-contest) (200-meter dash, discus throw, javelin throw, long jump, and wrestling),[4] the 400-meter race in armor, the 200-meter dash (*stadion*), the 400-meter race (*diaulos*), and the 4,800-meter race (*dolichos*). Victories in all these events (including many in the boys' division) are celebrated in Pindar's extant victory odes.

The most prestigious event was the four-horse chariot race. It required considerable wealth to keep horses in Greece, for pasturage was very limited, especially on the smaller islands. The owner of the horses was considered the winner, whoever the driver might be, just as today. Naturally, great and powerful men such as Hieron of Syracuse and Theron of Akragas would never risk their own lives in a race: they purchased and bred the horses, hired the trainers and drivers, and paid for the expenses of transport and upkeep—no small enterprise. The drivers do, however, come in for special notice in the odes, when there is something exceptional about them. Karrhotos, whom the scholia report as a kinsman of Arkesilas of Kyrene, is praised at length in *Pyth.* 5 for winning at the Pythian games out of a field of forty chariots. In fact, he dedicated his unscathed and obviously ornate chariot to the shrine at Delphi. Nikomachos, charioteer for Xenokrates of Akragas, is mentioned in *Isth.* 2 as particularly skillful. And Herodotos of Thebes, celebrated in *Isth.* I, actually drove his own chariot. If we include *Pyth.* 3, eighteen of the odes are to equestrian victors, and thirteen of these are for victors from Sicilian cities.

Of the odes to victors in gymnastic events, eight are for victories in the pankration, three in boxing, six in wrestling, two in the pentathlon, one in the race in armor, three in the *stadion*, two in the *diaulos*, and one in the *dolichos*.[5] Of these, eleven are to boy victors. Athletic training began early, sometimes under the supervision of professional trainers. We hear praise of four such trainers in the odes: Melesias, Menander (both from Athens), Ilas, and Orseas. The victory won by Alkimedon of Aigina in the boys' wrestling at Olympia (*Ol.* 8) is his trainer Melesias's thirtieth. In the Panathenaic games in Athens, there were prizes for first and second-place winners in men's, youths', and boys' categories.[6] These facts make it clear that these athletes were not simply part-time participants. Pindar stresses over and over the training, effort, and expense that go into achieving victory, and we see numerous examples of clans and families that devote themselves to athletics. In *Nem.* 6, the boy wrestler Alkimidas of Aigina has won his clan's twenty-fifth victory in the four major contests.

The victors. Pindar says of the delights of winning an Olympic crown: "for the rest of his life the victor enjoys a honey-sweet calm as far as games can give it" (*Ol.* 1.97–99). Here he is thinking primarily of the spiritual exultation of an Olympic victory that—come what else may—lasts throughout one's lifetime. But there were also material rewards for athletes. David Young has recently demonstrated that the prizes in the Panathenaic games were very valuable.[7] And, although there were no direct rewards for victories in the crown games, the victors enjoyed considerable prestige, preferment, and monetary rewards in their home polis. Already in the sixth century, legislation attributed to Solon limits the amount paid to Olympic victors in Athens at 500 drachmas and to Isthmian victors at 100; and in a poem Xenophanes (ca. 525 B.C.) complains about the preferential treatment athletes receive. An Athenian inscription of around 430 B.C. reads: "Those who have won gymnastic events at Olympia, Delphi, Isthmia, or Nemea shall have free meals in the town hall along with other personal honors. Likewise there shall be free meals in the town hall for all who have won (or win hereafter) with a team of four, team of two, or single horse at Olympia, Delphi, Isthmia, or Nemea" (IG^2 77.11–17). And in Plato's *Apology*, Sokrates ironically proposes as his penalty free meals in the town hall like an Olympic chariot victor.

In addition, the fame of an Olympic victor lived after him, and not only in poems such as Pindar composed. Statues, or even shrines, might commemorate him. The famous sophist Hippias of Elis (ca. 420 B.C.) compiled a list of Olympic victors and Aristotle himself made one of Pythian victors.[8] Both of these are lost, but we do have a list of all the winners in the stadion from 776 B.C. to 217 A.D. compiled by Sextus Julius Africanus.[9] One of the remarkable finds at Oxyrhynchus was a papyrus dating from about 250 A.D. that contains a list of Olympic victors in all the events (but the mule cart race) for the four Olympiads from 480 to 468 B.C. and the three from 456 to 448 B.C. Here is the entry for the 76th Olympiad in 476 B.C. (dashes indicate letters or names missing in the papyrus):[10]

> [76th. Ska]mandros of Mitylene, stadion
> [Da]ndis of Argos, diaulos
> [————] of Sparta, dolichos
> [————] of Taras, pentathlon
> [———— of Ma]roneia, wrestling
> [Euthymos of Lok]roi in Italy, boxing
> [Theagenes of Th]asos, pankration

[————] of Sparta, boys' stadion
[Theognetos of Aigi]na, boys' wrestling
[Hag]esi[da]mos of Lokroi in Italy, boys' boxing
[Ast]ylos of Syracuse, race in armor
[Ther]on of Akragas, owner, four horse chariot
[Hier]on of Syracuse, owner, single horse

This papyrus from a relatively small and out-of-the-way city in Egypt, which records victories won seven centuries before it was written, vividly demonstrates the enduring importance of athletics and the commemoration of victors throughout the Greek world. Five of Pindar's most impressive Olympian odes are composed for victors listed above: *Ol.* 1 for Hieron of Syracuse, *Ol.* 2 and 3 for Theron of Akragas, and *Ol.* 10 and 11 for Hagesidamos of Western (Italian) Lokroi. In addition, Dandis of Argos and Astylos of Syracuse were very famous athletes.[11] We have an epigram attributed to Simonides, Pindar's older contemporary, that was composed for the base of a statue commemorating Theognetos of Aigina:[12]

> Look and see Theognetos, the Olympic victor,
>   a boy who was a skillful charioteer of wrestling,
> most beautiful to behold, in action a match for his looks:
>   he crowned his noble fathers' city.

And finally, Theagenes (also spelled Theogenes) of Thasos was reported to have won some 1,300 victories, and was worshipped at a shrine in his native polis.[13]

What made these athletics so important to the Greeks? A complete answer is, of course, impossible, but several key terms can help point the way. The first are the words for the games themselves: *agōn* and *aethlos*. The first word stresses the striving, the action, the coming together in competition ("agony" and "antagonist" are derivatives). The second, from which our "athlete" and "athletics" come, stresses the prize (*aethlon*) the winner received. This prize also has two aspects: it can be material, as in the games in *Iliad* 23, or it can be immaterial, namely, fame among one's peers and in records, statues, and song. It is naturally the last that Pindar stresses. Another important term is *krisis* (judgment, decision), which Pindar uses several times to describe the games, for they are a form of trial or test in which rival claims are adjudicated by a judge. The judges at the Olympic games (*Hellanodikai*) were renowned for their accurate decisions, and in vase paintings

PINDAR

one often sees judges supervising competitions. A just judgment or
discrimination is essential in this competitive culture, for it is by
means of the *krisis* that superiority is determined. Greek life is full of
contests. For example, when the Athenians produced tragedies, they
made the event into a contest (*agōn*) in which judges determined first,
second, and third prizes. And finally, no analysis of Greek competitive
life could be complete without the term *aretē* (*areta* in Pindar's Doric
odes). It means, basically, "excellence" and implies the full use or realization of one's powers. A distinguishing characteristic of the Greek
spirit from Homer to Pindar and beyond is the constant striving for
areta, the full expression of human capability, achieved by superior
performance in the public realm. This view of life is essentially hier-
archical; the evaluative standard is the ideal of *areta*. Pindar sums up
many of these aspects at *Nem.* 7. 7–8, composed for a boy victor in the
pentathlon: "the son of Thearion, Sogenes, is famed in song because
he was distinguished (*kritheis,* judged) for his excellence (*aretāi*) among
pentathletes." Judgment, excellence, fame, song: Sogenes has been
tested and "distinguished"; his own name—and his father's—have
been preserved because of his *areta*; the other pentathletes remain forever anonymous.

The Epinician Genre

Pindar generally uses two terms to refer to his poems: *hymnos* (hymn)
and *aoida* (song).[14] The English word "ode" derives from the latter,
through the Attic form *ōdē*. Sometimes he also qualifies these terms
with the adjectives *epinikios* (for a victory; hence "epinician"), *kallinikos*
(triumphal) or *enkōmios* (celebratory). Taken together, all of these terms
define the primary intention of the genre: to praise victorious *areta* in
song. The epinician genre is basically a secularization of the hymn to
gods, where the emphasis shifts from praising the works and powers
of the gods (as in the Homeric hymns) to glorifying the achievements
of men. This shift parallels a general trend in Greek thought and art
of the period, which may be called "humanistic" or "secular," and can
also be seen in fifth-century sculpture, tragedy, and history. We noted
above that Eustathios accounted for the popularity of the victory odes
because they were "more concerned with human affairs." The Greek
word expresses well this overall tendency: *anthrōpikōteros* (more human-
centered).

But Pindar's odes are far from being completely secularized. There is not a single ode without a reference to the gods. The games were celebrated as part of a religious festival, and Pindar never loses sight of the divine realm. Indeed, he appears to be exceptionally pious; the bulk of his work was, after all, completely religious. Again and again, Pindar reminds his patrons that human achievement is entirely dependent upon the gods.

Simonides of Keos (ca. 556–468 B.C.) is credited with the invention of the epinician genre in the generation before Pindar. We know that he wrote poems for the Skopads of Thessaly and for powerful men in Sicily and southern Italy, but only a few fragments of them have survived. Interestingly, his odes were arranged according to the events celebrated, unlike the Pindaric classification by festivals. He reportedly traveled widely and became very wealthy. One story current in antiquity neatly illustrates the precarious balance that the epinician poet had to maintain between praising gods and patrons. According to the version in Cicero (*de Oratore* 2.352) Simonides wrote a poem in praise of Skopas of Thessaly in which he included a long section praising Kastor and Polydeukes; Skopas only gave him half of the promised fee and told him to get the rest from the two gods, since half the poem was devoted to them.[15] At times in Pindar as well, the victor seems to be dwarfed by praise of the gods.

The other important epinician poet was Bacchylides of Keos, the nephew of Simonides and a slightly younger contemporary of Pindar. In 1896 a papyrus was discovered in Egypt containing major portions of fourteen epinician odes and six dithyrambs. Three of these odes are to Hieron of Syracuse and one is to Pytheas of Aigina (also celebrated by Pindar in *Nem.* 5). It is evident that the two poets moved in the same circles, and the scholia hint at a rivalry between them, especially for the favor of Hieron and Theron. Thus when Pindar says in *Ol.* 2.86–88, "Wise is he who knows many things by nature; whereas learners that are loud and long-winded are like a pair of crows that vainly cry against the divine bird of Zeus," the scholia suggest that the two crows refer to Simonides and Bacchylides. Likewise, they see veiled references to Bacchylides throughout the last two triads of *Pyth.* 2 to Hieron. The texts are hard pressed to support such covert allusions to personal grudges, and recent scholars have been increasingly skeptical about their validity. We really know nothing certain about the relations between Pindar and Bacchylides.

The epinician genre was short-lived. These three poets constitute the beginning and end of the choral victory ode, which blossomed during Pindar's lifetime and suddenly died. The last epinician we hear of was composed by Euripides, when Alkibiades entered seven chariots in the Olympic games in 416 B.C. and won first, second, and third (some say fourth) place; only six verses survive.

Elements in the Victory Odes

Essential information. Simonides wrote many epigrams for victors, and one attributed to him succinctly states the "facts" of athletic victory (*Anth. Pal.* 16.23): "Tell your name, your father's, your city, your victory./Kasmylos, son of Euagoras, of Rhodes, boxing at Pytho." Although the father's name is optional, this is the essential information that was proclaimed at the games and contained in victor lists: name, city, event, games. It is fascinating to observe how Pindar relays that information. At times he refers to the victor by his own name, at others as the son of so-and-so. Sometimes he holds back one item so that he can introduce it at a climactic moment; at others he presents all the information at once. For example, the first sentence of *Pyth.* 9 conveys the basic facts about the victor in this order: race in armor, Pythian games, Telesikrates, of Kyrene. By saving the name of the city until the last word, he can then move right into a narrative about its legendary founder.

Ol. 13 provides an example of holding back one item. At line 1 we learn that the victor won at Olympia; at 4 we know that he is Corinthian; at line 28 we get his name, Xenophon; and finally at 30 we are told the event(s): he won an unprecedented double victory in the stadion and pentathlon. The first triad ends with this triumphant information. At other times, the facts are given piecemeal. For example, in *Ol.* 10 the first two lines provide two facts: "Read me the Olympic victor's name, Archestratos's son." In line 13 we learn that the city in question is Western Lokroi (in Italy), and at 16–18 we discover that the event was boxing, that the victor's trainer was Ilas, and that his own name is Hagesidamos. By mentioning the trainer, Pindar also informs us that Hagesidamos won in the boys' division. Pindar is a master at making this otherwise prosaic information an integral part of his poems.

Pindar also uses another means to give variety and life to the facts: allusive references. These oblique references are especially common for place names and are one of the stumbling blocks for the beginning reader. For example, any of the following allusions would immediately tell his Greek audience that he was talking about Olympia: Pisa (the town nearest Olympia), Alpheos (the river at Olympia), the Hill of Kronos (the highest hill at Olympia), or "greatest games of Zeus." The following refer to the Pythian games: Delphi or Pytho (the site of the games), Krisa or Kirrha (nearby towns), Kastalia (the spring), Parnassos (the adjacent mountain), or the "games of Apollo." Nemea can be the "vale of the lion," an allusion to the Nemean lion that Herakles slew, while the Isthmos can be called the "bridge" at Corinth. Once these circumlocutions are mastered, Pindar's artful use of them becomes apparent.

Hymnal elements. As we mentioned above, the epinician ode is an adaptation of a hymn to a god. Pindar frequently refers to his odes as *hymnoi* and hymnal elements abound in them. Many begin with elaborate hymns to various deities, such as Olympia (*Ol.* 8), Fortune (*Ol.* 12), the Graces (*Ol.* 14), the Lyre (*Pyth.* 1), Peace (*Pyth.* 8), Eleithyia, goddess of birth (*Nem.* 7), Hora, goddess of adolescence (*Nem.* 8), Theia, mother of the sun (*Isth.* 5), and Theba (*Isth.* 7). Some of these deities are nymphs who bear the name of a city or place: Olympia and Theba; others are what we in a monotheistic culture would call "abstractions": the Lyre, Peace, Theia (the principle of light); others are minor deities in Greek polytheistic religion: Fortune, the Graces, Eleithyia, and Hora.[16] The major gods in the Greek pantheon, such as Zeus, Apollo, Poseidon, and Athena, are constantly mentioned in the odes, but there are no hymns to them on the scale of those cited above. Pindar's world is full of divinities; Kyrene, for example, is at once the city in north Africa and the nymph who married Apollo and became the patron goddess of the city. All aspects of human life, such as birth, youth, marriage, death, success, fortune, knowledge, beauty, health, and happiness, depend upon the action of gods, sometimes specifically mentioned, often simply designated as *theos* (god) or *daimōn* (divinity).

A detailed discussion of hymnal style is beyond the scope of this book,[17] but a brief survey of the typical elements found in hymns will help the reader make sense of Pindar's procedures. In general, classical hymns consist of some (rarely all) of the following parts: (1) an invocation that includes (a) the god's name; (b) appropriate adjectives ("epithets"); (c) genealogy; (d) location; (e) sphere of influence, powers ("aretalogy"); (2) a request that can be lengthy or a mere command like "hear me"; (3) in addition, any of the above can be expanded by means of (a) a relative clause (e.g., "you who . . ."); (b) explanations (e.g., "because you . . ."); (c) examples, sometimes extended narratives; (d) reminders of the god's (or worshipper's) service or devotion.

For example, *Nem.* 11 begins with a hymn to Hestia (goddess of the hearth) on the occasion of Aristagoras's installment as chief councilman for his city Tenedos. It can be broken up into the following elements:

Daughter of Rhea,	(genealogy)
you who control city halls,	(relative clause giving her powers)
Hestia,	(name)
sister of highest Zeus and of Hera who shares his throne,	(genealogy, epithets and location for Zeus and Hera)
welcome Aristagoras into your chamber and welcome his companions beside your glorious scepter.	(request)
By honoring you they keep Tenedos upright, and worship you first of gods with many libations and many sacrifices.	(reminder of the worshippers' devotion to the god)

Hestia represents the ancient and universal principles of good government in a universe ruled by her brother Zeus. Her symbols of office are the "chamber" and "scepter." With her help the new magistrate hopes to guide his city properly. The hymn links gods and men in joint effort for the good of the community, which is bound together by the symbol of the "hearth," protected by Hestia.[18]

The first strophe of *Nem.* 7 to Sogenes of Aigina contains a splendid hymn of thanksgiving to Eleithyia, goddess of childbirth, for making possible his victory.

> Eleithyia, enthroned beside the deep-counseling Fates,
> daughter of great-strengthed Hera, hear me, goddess of childbirth.
> Without you, we behold neither the light nor dark of night,
> nor do we come to have your sister, bright-limbed Youth.
> Yet, the breath of life is not the same for all of us,
> for the yoke of each man's destiny limits him in different ways.
> By your grace, however, Thearion's son, Sogenes, is famed in song
> because he was distinguished for his excellence among pentathletes.

This hymn contains most of the elements listed above. Eleithyia, childbirth, represents a sine qua non of existence, the common link of all men who draw breath in this world of day and night. And although we are similar in the fact of our birth and development to youth, our individual lives are qualitatively different. Sogenes has succeeded where others have failed. There must have been something at his birth that marked him for success. When we recall that Eleithyia takes her place beside the Fates and is the daughter of Hera, we realize that her activity is part of a much larger scheme of order that includes destiny and Hera's influence. Through Eleithyia's agency Sogenes has realized his youthful *areta*. God and man must work together; without divine help there is no existence; with it there can even be success.

Pindar's opening hymns portray the universal conditions within which the present occasion is a specific instance. They provide a context that makes the event being celebrated meaningful. The movement is always from general to specific, until an individual man is singled out. Out of all the men who have been born, each with the limitations of his own destiny, the young man Sogenes has been distinguished in his own way. Likewise, in *Ol.* 12 Pindar hymns the powers of Fortune (Tycha), who controls the outcome of men's affairs. She reverses expectations and brings now pain and then pleasure; meanwhile, men cannot foresee how any action will turn out. Ergoteles of Himera is then introduced as a specific example of Fortune's unexpected ways. He suffered exile from his native Krete, but it turned out to be a blessing, as he is now an Olympic victor for his new city, Himera in Sicily. His pain has turned to joy, his obscurity to fame. Pindar speaks of "joining" the victor to a hymn in praise of gods (*Isth.* 1.16), and this well describes his general procedure.

Prayers.   Prayers are closely related to hymns but are less elaborate and are essentially requests. There are dozens of prayers throughout the odes that ask for the gods' goodwill and continued blessings. Sometimes the poet prays for assistance in his task; often his prayer is for the victor or city he is celebrating. The function of these prayers is inevitably transitional. They signal a beginning, a change of subject, or conclusion, much as they still do in Christian liturgical practice. These prayers, of course, also serve as reminders that the occasion is a solemn and religious one. [19]

Gnomes.   *Gnōmē* is the Greek word for maxim, pithy saying (Latin, *sententia*). We have seen that the highly developed lyric poetry of Pindar borrows many elements from the hymnal tradition. It also borrows from an earlier didactic tradition which includes Hesiod (especially the *Works and Days*), Theognis, Phokylides, and a lost work

containing the "sayings of Cheiron" (the legendary centaur who edu-
cated Jason, Achilles, and Asklepios) upon which Pindar undoubtedly
drew. Aphorisms abound in the odes, such as "the days to come are
the wisest witnesses," "trial is the test of men," "in a single space of
time winds shift now here, now there," "all credit is due the inventor,"
"it is impossible to conceal inborn character," "one must praise the
good," and "exhaust the means at hand."

Like prayers, gnomes tend to articulate parts of an ode, but Pindar
uses them whenever he wishes to add a universal dimension to his
subject. They also serve as counsel and provide a serious ethical and
practical aspect to the praise. The hymns and prayers in the odes emphasize the poet's role as priestly spokesman for the gods; the gnomes
designate his role as teacher and counsellor. Pindar is a master of these
sayings, and often they are so compressed that they are difficult to
unravel. This is the side of Pindar to be found in such collections of
quotations as Bartlett's.

Mythical narrative.   Pindar's debt to the epic tradition, represented by Homer, Hesiod, the Homeric Hymns, and epic poems no
longer extant, is most obvious in his narratives. The stories that Pindar
tells, loosely called "myths," are taken from the great fund of Hellenic
legend and have been of great interest to students of religion, mythol-
ogy, and narrative technique. Often the stories concern heroes connected with the victor's family or city, and most deal positively with
their subject. These myths set the victory in a wider context and illustrate qualities that the poet recommends in his subject. But Pindar
will also use a story to convey a warning or to illustrate qualities opposite from those he is praising. Such "negative examples" occur in *Ol.*
1 (the story of Tantalos), *Pyth.* 1 (Typhon), *Pyth.* 2 (Ixion), *Pyth.* 3
(Koronis and Asklepios), and *Pyth.* 11 (Klytaimestra).

Ring-composition.   A very important narrative technique borrowed
from epic poetry is "ring-composition."[20] The most famous Homeric
example is in the nineteenth book of the *Odyssey*, when the old nurse
washes the disguised Odysseus and discovers his scar. At line 392 "she
recognized the scar," but it is not until line 468 that the startled nurse
"lets drop his foot." In the intervening lines, Homer tells the history
of the scar, and his procedure is worth examining in some detail. By
means of a series of relative and temporal clauses, he rapidly sketches
the coming story by progressively moving backward in time. It was
the scar *that* the boar inflicted, *when* Odysseus had gone to visit his
grandfather, *who* had named him when he was born. Within a few

lines, the poet has outlined the story from the present (the nurse sees the scar) back to Odysseus's infancy. At this point Homer expatiates on each of these events in reverse order in the next sixty verses until he arrives at the present moment when the nurse drops the foot.

Many myths in Pindar are subtle variations of ring-composition. Sometimes the poet gives a summary statement of the coming story,[21] then fills in the details, and returns (often with different, but echoing, vocabulary) to the opening summary. For example, the brief "myth" in *Pyth.* 6 begins with the general topic: Antilochos died for his father by awaiting the attack of Memnon the Aithiopian. Pindar then fills in the details of this heroic action and concludes with the statement: "and he waited there and bought his father's rescue at the price of his own death." Pindar reinforces the sense of completion by echoing the words "awaiting," "waited" and "died," "death."[22]

We will point out other examples of ring-composition when analyzing individual odes, so let us take an example from one that will not be treated in detail. At the opening of *Pyth.* 9, the poet announces that his song will be a crown for Kyrene. He then rapidly sketches the coming narrative with a relative pronoun: *whom* Apollo once snatched from Pelion and took to north Africa, *where* Aphrodite welcomed them, her (Kyrene) *who* from the time of her birth was not interested in women's chores. From this point we proceed forward in time, with scenes of Kyrene guarding her father's flocks and of Apollo falling in love with her when he sees her fighting with a lion and asking Cheiron's advice on whether or not to have intercourse with her. The centaur (after teasing Apollo for asking what as god of prophecy he should already know) predicts marriage and the birth of a son, Aristaios. Here (as often) the narrative continues beyond the completed "ring," and includes vivid scenes, interesting in their own right.

Scenes. Another important aspect of Pindar's narrative technique is the selection of "scenes" or "tableaux," which he depicts almost as if he were describing a vase painting or sculptural group. The above myths from *Pyth.* 6 and 9 portray scenes that could easily be painted. Another good example is Herakles' strangulation of the snakes in *Nem.* 1.[23] In her wrath, Hera sends two snakes to kill the infant Herakles in his crib during the night, but the prodigious child grasps each one by the throat and holds them until they expire. Meanwhile, hearing the commotion, the handmaids are terrified, while Alkmena, Herakles' mother, leaps out of bed without her gown and tries to ward off the attacking snakes; the Theban chieftains rush in fully armed along with

Amphitryon, Herakles' father, who stands there brandishing his drawn
sword in terrified anticipation. The moment is caught as if in a snap-
shot. We can easily visualize the scene: the women are in panic, while
Alkmena is the center of attention as she tries to fight off the snakes;
meanwhile, the armed men rush in, with Amphitryon brandishing his
sword. In the center is the crib with the two infants, Herakles and his
twin brother Iphikles. Everything is portrayed in pairs: the handmaids,
the men at arms; Alkmena, Amphitryon; Herakles and Iphikles; even
the pair of snakes. Specific details also reinforce the pairing of the
parents: Alkmena jumps out of bed without her gown (*apeplos*), while
Amphitryon's sword is "naked" (*gymnos*); both are singled out of their
respective groups by their impetuous haste. One can even visualize
contrasts of light and shade: the dark bedroom at night flashing with
bronze armor and weapons. And in this moment, held before our eyes,
we are told that Amphitryon's initial anguish turned to joy as he beheld
the divine strength of his son. The scene captures that instant of wondrous discovery, the recognition of divine powers at work. Against the
backdrop of commotion, Amphitryon becomes the center of focus; we
can almost see the changing expression on his face. This ability to
select the telling instance (*kairos*) is a mark of all great Greek art and
literature.

   Other famous scenes in the odes are the prayer of Pelops in *Ol.* 1,
the isle of the blessed in *Ol.* 2, the birth of Iamos in *Ol.* 6, the rest-
fulness of the gods in contrast to the eruption of Mt. Aitna in *Pyth.* 1,
Apollo rescuing his son Asklepios from the burning pyre in *Pyth.* 3,
the appearance of Jason in *Pyth.* 4, the discussion of Apollo and Cheiron as they watch the nymph Kyrene in *Pyth.* 9, the dialogue with
Zeus when Polydeukes saves his brother Kastor in *Nem.* 10, Herakles'
prayer for Telamon's son in *Isth.* 6, and Themis addressing the gods in
Isth. 8. There are numerous others as well. At the beginning of *Nem.*
5, Pindar declares that he is no maker of statues that sit on their bases,
but he certainly has an eye for visual representation and borrows many
techniques from painters and sculptors.

   Catalogs.   The odes abound with catalogs—lists of victories,
heroes, places, people, and virtuous qualities. They are a mark of Pindar's comprehensive vision. The reader of the odes in translation may
initially find them perfunctory, but in Greek they are one of the wonders of Pindar's style. He obviously took great pains to vary and enliven
them, and his ability to do so under such demanding metrical con-
straints is amazing. He never simply repeats names, but uses circum-

locutions and oblique references, varies the terms, changes the pace, switches from negative to positive expressions, employs metaphors, and breaks up the order with digressions. Pindar never gives the impression of composing his catalogs mechanically; on the contrary, each catalog is uniquely crafted for its ode and is a masterpiece in its own right. These catalogs ultimately derive from prose lists such as the inventories found on Linear B tablets and on papyri, but in Pindar's poetry they become virtuoso performances.[24]

Priamels. Twentieth-century scholars have recognized a certain poetic form called a "priamel" (pronounced pree-á-mel)[25] that is prominent in Pindar and occurs throughout classical literature. The term is a German word deriving from the Latin *praeambulum* (prelude, introduction). As it applies to classical literature, a priamel consists of two parts: "foil" and "climax." The function of the foil is to introduce and highlight the climactic term by enumerating other examples, subjects, times, places, or instances, which then yield (with varying degrees of contrast or analogy) to the particular point of interest or importance. Sometimes the other items are listed in catalogs; sometimes they are summarized with words such as "many," "various," or "some."

These focusing devices can achieve many subtle effects. For example, *Ol.* 11 opens with a priamel that occupies the strophe:

> There are times when men most need winds;
> there are times when they need heavenly waters,
> drenching children of the cloud.
> But if a man succeeds through toil, honey-sounding hymns
> become a foundation for future fame
> and a faithful testimony to great achievements (*aretais*).
>
> (1–6)

This priamel consists of three elements: (1) need for winds (one thinks of sailing); (2) need for rain (one thinks of farmers); and (3) need for song. Each statement is longer than the preceding one. It is obvious that the first two examples are "foil," for the poet is not really interested in navigation and farming except as background to show how achievement needs to be celebrated in song if it is to survive in fame. The word "but" (*de*) and the change of syntax signal the climactic term. Thus, "there are times when" song, too, takes its place among the basic needs of man, and of course the present occasion is one of them.

Pindar states the same idea more succinctly at *Nem.* 3.6–8:

> Various activities thirst for different things,
> but athletic victory most loves song,
> the ablest attendant for crowns and achievements (*aretan*).

In the summary expression "various . . . different" we are free to supply concrete items; the verb "thirst" suggests strong craving. But (*de*) victory "loves" song most of all. There is yet another priamel on the same theme at *Isth.* 1.47, where the poet begins with a summary statement: "Men enjoy different rewards for different tasks." He then amplifies this general observation with four specific examples, shepherd, ploughman, fowler, and fisherman, all of whom represent man's basic quest for nourishment. This list is followed by the climactic statement that the reward for success in athletics or war is praise, clearly the subject of real interest, for Pindar then proceeds to praise the victor for his athletic achievements. These three priamels, each in its own way, define relationships between achievement (*areta*) and song. In the first, *areta* "needs" song (as sailors need wind and farmers rain); in the second, *areta* "loves" song; in the third, *areta* seeks song as a "reward" (as the shepherd, etc., work for food). By providing an analogous context, these priamels give depth and force to their ideas.

Other priamels of note in Pindar include the catalog of places where heroes are celebrated, which culminates with Aigina and the sons of Aiakos (*Isth.* 5.30–35):

> In the splendid sacrifices of the Aitolians
> the mighty sons of Oineus are honored;
> while in Thebes it is horse-driving Iolaos,
> and Perseus in Argos, and the spearmen Kastor and
>   Polydeukes by the streams of Eurotas.
> But in Aigina it is the great-hearted spirits of
> Aiakos and his sons.

Another is the hymn to Theba which opens *Isth.* 7 and contains a list of Theban glories that is capped with the recent victory of Strepsiades in the pankration. Still other examples will be noted in the course of analyses of individual odes. But perhaps the most famous example of a priamel in Pindar is the splendid opening of *Ol.* 1:

> Best is water, but then gold, like fire gleaming at night,
> outshines all other lordly wealth.
> But if it is athletics

> you intend to praise, my heart,
> then look no further than the sun
> for another daytime star with warmer light in the empty sky,
> nor let us praise a contest greater than Olympia.
>
> (1–7)

Behind this priamel is the question "What is best?" Answers are given from various categories. Water is best for sustenance, gold is the best form of wealth, but the subject of ultimate interest is Olympia, best of all the games. Each member is longer than the previous one (as in the priamel in *Ol.* 11). The second and third elements contain embedded similes, and the second simile is longer than the first. These similes also show an intensification from fire shining at night to the splendor of the sun in broad daylight. There is, as well, an implicit progression from the material aspects of existence (water as sustenance and gold as wealth), to the realm of action (athletics).[26] It is easy to see why an ode with this glorious beginning would be placed first in the collection. It is also easy to see why the richness and complexity of Pindar's language has baffled readers first coming to Pindar.[27]

These elements are the principal "building blocks" of Pindar's odes. The attentive reader, especially of the Greek, will discover that Pindar never gives the impression of using them in a mechanical, careless way, but always varies them, so that they are perfectly adapted to their particular ode and interesting in their own right. Often he combines them. For example, in the above passage from *Isth.* 5.30–35, a catalog of people and places is structured as a priamel. Opening hymns often function as a priamel, as in the case of *Ol.* 12, where the "many" (see ll. 6, 10) surprises that Fortune brings are given concrete expression in the career of the victor, Ergoteles of Himera. Perhaps the most spectacular combination of elements occurs in the hymn to Theba at *Isth.* 7.1–21, which consists of a hymn, a catalog, a priamel, and even a gnome. Throughout the odes, Pindar interweaves these elements to form one complex whole, much as any great composer joins together basic musical elements in ever-new arrangements.[28]

Chapter Four
The Odes to Hieron

Pindar's greatest patron was Hieron of Syracuse, the king (tyrant) of the most powerful city in Sicily. Hieron was the second of four sons of Deinomenes, the cavalry commander in Gela, a city about seventy-five miles from Syracuse. The others were Gelon, Polyzalos, and Thrasyboulos. In 491 Gelon became tyrant of Gela and in 485 took over rule of Syracuse, leaving Hieron as viceroy in Gela. When Gelon died in 478, Hieron succeeded him as tyrant of Syracuse. Hieron was a great patron of the arts, who entertained and commissioned works from Simonides, Bacchylides, Aischylos (who wrote a play, *Aetnai*, to celebrate his founding of the city Aitna), and of course Pindar. Hieron was devoted to horse racing, a sport in which the Sicilians excelled. The famous *Charioteer of Delphi* (reproduced on the frontispiece to this volume) is all that remains of a group riding in a chariot, dedicated by Hieron's brother Polyzalos, probably when he was tyrant of Gela. A rock slide buried it at Delphi and preserved a fitting complement in sculpture to the severe dignity of Pindar's odes.

Four major poems to Hieron are preserved in the collection of epinician odes; we also have fragments of an enkomion to him, and there may well have been others that are lost. Two of the epinician odes are firmly dated: *Ol.* 1 in 476 and *Pyth.* 1 in 470. The occasions of the other two (*Pyth.* 2 and 3) are much in doubt.

One of the striking features of these odes is their variety. Each is remarkably distinct from the others. Two are composed in Aeolic meter (*Ol.* 1 and *Pyth.* 2) and two are in Doric dactylo-epitritic (*Pyth.* 1 and 3). All are different in their form, organization, tone, and subject matter. We shall begin with a close analysis of *Pyth.* 1 and 3, perhaps the most accessible of Pindar's great odes, in order to demonstrate the intricate workings of a Pindaric ode and to lay a foundation for briefer analyses of the other poems.

Pythian 1.[1]   The ode opens with an elaborate hymn to the lyre:

Strophe 1
Golden Lyre, possession of Apollo and the violet-haired Muses
that acts as their spokesman, to you the footstep listens

as it begins the splendid celebration,
while the singers heed your signals,
whenever your vibrations strike up the choir-leading preludes.
You quench even the thunderbolt's spear
of eternal fire. And the eagle sleeps on the scepter of Zeus,
    relaxing his swift wings at his sides,

Antistrophe 1

that king of birds, when you have shed over his curved head
a black-hooded cloud, sweet seal for his eyelids. And as he slumbers,
he ripples his smooth back, held in check
by your volley of notes. Yes, even violent Ares puts aside
his sharp-pointed spears and delights his heart
in sleep. And your shafts also soothe the minds of the gods,
    through the skill of Leto's son and the deep-breasted Muses.

                                                                    (1–12)

The movement is slow and steady. Here is the meter of the first two lines: — u — —/— u — —/— u u — u u —; — u — —/— u u — /— u — —/— u u — u u —/— —. The divisions distinguish the epitritic units (— u — —) from the dactylic (— u u). The periods (lines) in this poem are very long; the last one in each strophe and antistrophe contains thirty syllables and is the longest in the odes.[2]

The hymn begins with an invocation by naming the personified Lyre. The epithet "golden" can be taken literally, but metaphorically it indicates the superlative quality of this divine instrument. In lieu of a genealogy, the Lyre is the possession of the choirmaster Apollo and his choral entourage, the Muses, for whom it is a "spokesman" or advocate; its "location" is with them. The relative clause beginning with "to you" (2) introduces the Lyre's powers and spheres of influence. These will be the subject of the remainder of the hymn. The Lyre's first "power" is to lead the dancing and singing; and in performance the audience would actually see what was being described in the ode and hear the divine lyre's counterpart in the actual one being played.

In line 5, we suddenly shift to the divine realm, where a series of tableaux define the powers of the Lyre in terms of its effects on other people or things.[3] The thunderbolt and eagle are symbols of Zeus's power. Pindar treats the first briefly, but expands his description of the eagle to five lines that continue into the antistrophe. He clearly delights in this leisurely portrayal, with its visual details that allow one to picture the eagle relaxing—but visibly breathing—on the scepter of Zeus. Two different metaphors portray the effects of the Lyre's music on the eagle. First, it sheds a cloud over its head like a falcon's hood that is "sweet" and calming; but then its notes are like "volleys" of weapons. Even violent Ares (god of war) puts aside his spears. This scene is full of tension. Pindar never lets us forget that the relaxation created by the Lyre's music is momentary, and to a great extent this is accomplished through his use of adjectives. The thunderbolt's fire is "eternal," the eagle's wings are "swift," Ares is "violent" and his spears are "sharp." These are not merely decorative; they remind us that the thunderbolt is never entirely extinguished, that those smooth wings and curved head of the eagle can suddenly burst into swift and powerful action, and that Ares' natural place is in the din of battle.

Pindar then widens the focus to include the soothing effects on the rest of the gods,[4] and rounds off this portion of the hymn by "ringing" with the beginning. The last phrase "of Leto's son (i.e., Apollo) and the deep-breasted Muses" (12) clearly echoes "of Apollo and the violet-haired Muses" (1–2). The fact that the ringing line comes at the end of the antistrophe also helps to give a sense of closure. In addition to its soothing effects there is a hint of violence in the Lyre's music as well: its "volleys" hold the eagle in check and its "shafts" sooth the minds of the gods. This surprising aspect of song will become clearer when we see its effects on its enemies:

Epode 1

But those creatures without Zeus's love are terrified
when they hear the shout of the Pierian Muses, those on land
   and in the overpowering sea,
and especially the one lying in dreadful Tartaros, enemy of the gods,
Typhon the hundred-headed, who was once reared
in that famous Kilikian cave, but now
the sea-fencing cliffs above Kyma
and Sicily weigh upon his shaggy chest,
   and a skyward column constrains him,
snowy Mt. Aitna, year-round nurse of biting snow.

(13–20)

Suddenly Pindar presents another aspect of his theme. There was no way to have predicted that he would do this; he could have ended his hymn to the Lyre at this point and gone on to a peaceful celebration of the present occasion. But once he introduces this new aspect, the sphere of the song widens, and eventually we shall come to see the appropriateness of this apparent digression.

From Heaven we descend to Hell for a dark mirror image. The same song of the Lyre that relaxed the assembly of the gods in the company of Zeus is experienced as a terrifying "shout" or war cry[5] by those creatures that do not have Zeus's favor. Pindar begins with the vague expression "those creatures," then surveys the land and sea, and finally narrows the focus to Typhon in Tartaros (Hell). This primeval monster, "enemy of the gods," was the last challenge to Zeus's reign.[6] He is depicted as pinned down by the "cliffs above Kyma" (i.e., Mt. Vesuvius on the Bay of Naples) and "snowy Mt. Aitna (Etna)." Both of these are active volcanoes, and although the two places—Kyma and Aitna—are mentioned in passing, they will become very important in the course of the ode.

Ostensibly, Typhon was introduced to show the power of the Lyre over all creation, including Zeus's enemies. But as the account proceeds, the opening hymn drops out of sight, as Pindar embarks on one of his characteristic "digressions." The first triad has provided a panoramic sweep from Heaven, across land and sea, to Tartaros, and the epode ends with a vision of snow-clad Mt. Aitna towering to the sky. The poet then pauses for a full-scale description (*ekphrasis* in Greek rhetorical terms) of the eruption of Mt. Aitna, a theme that became famous in antiquity.[7]

Strophe 2

From its depths belch forth holiest springs
of unapproachable fire. By day its rivers
 pour forth a blazing stream of smoke,
but at night the tumbling red flame
carries boulders into the deep expanse of the sea
 with a crash.
That monster sends up those terrible springs
of Hephaistos's fire—an awesome portent to behold,
 a wonder even to hear about from witnesses,

Antistrophe 2

such is that creature confined between Aitna's dark-leaved peaks
and the plain, as his jagged bed goads the entire length
 of his outstretched back.
                                                            (21–28)

The leisurely description of the eagle asleep on Zeus's scepter (the symbol of power under the control of kingly rule) is paralleled by the even more expansive description of Typhon's violent eruptions (symbol of power controlled only by physical force). Pindar pulls out all the stops in this passage, and we have already noted the sound effects of the alliterated *p*'s in line 24.[8] Unlike the calm scene in heaven that was neatly rounded off with the echoing phrase "Apollo and the Muses," this scene rises to an emotional climax of astonishment: "awesome portent," "a wonder," "such is that creature." We have come a long way from the opening hymn; the audience must wonder what this ode is really about; the poet must somehow get to his proper subject. To do this he uses a prayer:

> Grant us, O Zeus, favor in your sight,
> you who rule this mountain, the forehead
>   of a fruitful land, whose neighboring city that bears its name
> was honored by its glorious founder,
> when at Pytho's racecourse the herald proclaimed it
>   as he announced Hieron's victory

Epode 2

with the chariot.

(29–33)

This prayer, uttered suddenly upon the contemplation of this terrible sight, asks that the poet and others like him may find favor with Zeus; that is, be leagued with the power and order of Zeus, Apollo, and the Muses. Now that the positive note is struck, Pindar quickly provides the "essential information." The herald at the Pythian games has announced Hieron of Aitna as winner of the chariot race.[9] That "neighboring city that bears its name" is the city of Aitna (modern Catania), founded by Hieron in 476/5. At this point, the detailed description of Mt. Aitna has more relevance; the erupting volcano is the backdrop for this new city, heralded at the Pythian games.[10] We have finally arrived at the occasion of the ode; from now on the poet will, in one way and another, praise Aitna's "glorious founder":

> First blessing for sailors when setting out
> on a voyage is the coming of a favoring wind, since it augurs well
> for a more prosperous return at the end. And this saying,
> given this present success, inspires the expectation that the city
> will hereafter be famous for its crowns and its horses,
> and be celebrated in tuneful feasts.

Lykian Apollo, ruler of Delos, you who love
  the Kastalian spring on Mt. Parnassos,
graciously take this to heart and make this a land of good men.
                                                        (33–40)

These lines are concerned with the continued well-being of the new city. After appealing to the proverbial wisdom of "good start, good finish,"[11] the poet prays that Apollo will vouchsafe its future success. Significantly, Apollo "loves" the Kastalian spring. Forms of the word *philos* (love, friendship) appear seven times in the ode at important places. We have already seen the condition of those creatures "without Zeus's love" (*pephilēke*) at line 13. Also, since the victory was won at Delphi, it is fitting that Pindar emphasize Apollo's fondness for the Kastalian spring. This prayer completes the second triad and the praise of the city. We await further word on its "glorious founder."

Strophe 3

For the gods provide all the means for human achievements,
be it inborn wisdom, or strength of hand and eloquence.
    In my eagerness to praise
that man, I hope
not to throw, like an athlete, the bronze-cheeked javelin
    whirling from my hand outside the boundary,
but to cast it far beyond my competitors'.
May all time to come continue to grant him
    such happiness and prosperity,
    and make him forget his hardships.
                                                        (41–46)

Hieron was mentioned in passing in line 32 (in the genitive case). This strophe begins to focus on "that man," but it does so gradually. Following the prayer to Apollo in lines 39–40, the poet observes that the gods make possible "all" the means for human achievements (*aretais*). This summary statement is then specified by three categories of god-given talents: wisdom, strength, and eloquence. These three comprise the intellectual, physical, and political virtues necessary for making Aitna a "land of good men" (*euandron chōran*, 40). Pindar intends to use all of his talent to praise "that man," but is concerned that his enthusiasm may lead him to overdo it; he needs, as it were, a long but accurate throw. Through this athletic simile, the poet neatly alludes to the games that provide the occasion of the ode, but he also

engages the audience in sympathetic appreciation of his task. The poet/
athlete metaphor appears constantly in the odes and reminds us that
the poet is a performer too, and must rise to the occasion.[12] In this
case, we are meant to appreciate both his eagerness and the difficulty
of his subject; he too can win or lose.

Hieron's praise is introduced by a prayer for continued blessings,
which ends with an ominous reference to past "hardships." The poet
suggests that Hieron has had to endure suffering to arrive at his position; the coming praise will explain this in more detail:

Antistrophe 3

Surely it would recall those wars and battles,
in which he stood his ground with steady soul,
    and with divine help he and his family won
such honor as no other Greek has reaped
to crown his wealth with esteem. But now,
    like another Philoktetes,
he has taken to the field, when even the proud man
was compelled to seek his friendship. They say
    that the god-like heroes came to fetch him
    from Lemnos, wasting from his wound,

Epode 3

Poias's archer son,
who destroyed Priam's city and ended
    the Greeks' toils.
He walked on weak flesh, but he fulfilled his destiny.
In like fashion may god sustain Hieron
in time to come, and give him due measure
    of his desires.

                                                            (47–57)

This praise of Hieron opens and closes with prayers, and the echo of
"in time to come" (57) with "may all time to come" (46) adds a sense
of closure to this section, providing a good example of prayers and
ring-composition working together to articulate an ode. The historical
allusions are vague. We really know too little about the continuous
warfare in Sicily to pin down the precise references, but surely among
those "wars and battles" is the Battle of Himera, when in 480 Gelon,
Hieron's older brother, joined forces with Theron of Akragas to defeat
a massive Carthaginian army. Later in the ode Pindar will praise this
battle by name. The other, more recent campaign, when he went to

the aid of others like a Philoktetes, is more difficult, and could include either the Battle of Kyma in 474 (described in 72–75) or his assistance to Western Lokroi (mentioned in *Pyth*. 2.18–20), or both.[13]

The allusion to Philoktetes requires some explanation. At the beginning of the expedition against Troy, Philoktetes, the son of Poias, was bitten on the foot by a snake. The Greek commanders were unable to stand his suffering and abandoned him on the island of Lemnos. When all efforts to take Troy proved futile, they were forced to retrieve Philoktetes, for Troy was destined to fall to him with the aid of his bow. The scholia cite Aristotle as mentioning that Hieron suffered from kidney stones and add that he was carried to battle on a litter. Perhaps something of this sort is alluded to. But far more important is the fact that proud men sought his friendship, that he "ended the Greeks' toils," and that he fulfilled his destiny. Likewise, Hieron is the man of the hour for his fellow Greeks in desperate straits, a man who wages war unwillingly, but out of "friendship" (*philon*, 52).

At this point, it is well to recapitulate. After a splendid hymn to the powers of the lyre and a digression on Mt. Aitna, Hieron's victory in the Pythian games is mentioned and he and his family are praised for their wealth and martial successes. In a way, the ode is complete, for the victor has been named and praised. Yet several questions remain unanswered. What about this new city of Aitna so prominently introduced? What are the names of those battles hinted at in lines 47–55? We know of Hieron's generalship, but what about his qualities as ruler of his city? And finally, what is the significance of the grand hymn to the Lyre?

In line 58, the address to the Muse points the ode in a new—and unforeseen—direction. The poet turns to Hieron's son, Deinomenes (named for his grandfather), and asks the Muse to help him sing a "loving (*philion*) hymn" for Deinomenes, who is called Aitna's king, since Hieron has put him in charge of the new city.

> Muse, I beg you to include Deinomenes too in the celebration
> of this chariot victory, for the joy of his father's success
>   is as his own.
> Join me, then, in composing a loving hymn for Aitna's king.

Strophe 4

> His city was founded in divinely based freedom
> by Hieron under the laws of Hyllos's rule. For the descendants
>   of Pamphylos

and of Herakles' sons, who dwell
under the slopes of Mt. Taugetos, are determined to retain
   the institutions of Aigimios and remain
Doric. Their prosperous ancestors came down
from Mt. Pindos and took Amyklai, to become
   glorious neighbors of the white-horsed Tyndarids;
   and the fame of their spears flourished.

(58–66)

Strophe 4 is probably the least interesting to modern readers. It describes the Doric peoples who brought their institutions from Mt. Pindos in Thessaly to Amyklai just south of Sparta below Mt. Taugetos, where the Tyndarids (i.e., Kastor and Polydeukes) were worshipped. Hieron settled Aitna with some 5,000 immigrants from the Peloponnesos, who are to maintain their Doric traditions. Although it is a new city, its institutions are ancient, and Pindar prays that its people may thrive forever in their new location "by the waters of the Amenas" and that they may enjoy internal peace and freedom from outside aggression:

Antistrophe 4

Zeus, you who determine the end of all, may men's true report
always ascribe such good fortune as this to the citizens and their
   king by the waters of the Amenas.
For with your help, a ruler may,
with his son as viceroy, honor his people and turn them
   to harmonious peace.
I beseech you, son of Kronos, make the
Phoenicians and Etruscans keep their war cry
   quietly at home, now that they have seen their aggression
   bring woe to their fleet before Kyma,

Epode 4

such defeat did they suffer at the hands of the Syracusians' chief,
when he cast their youth from their swift ships into the sea
and delivered Greece from grievous slavery. I shall earn
the Athenians' favor as my reward by telling of Salamis
and the Spartans' by telling of the battles before Mt. Kithairon,
when the curve-bowed Persians were beaten;
but beside the well-watered banks of the Himeras

Deinomenes' sons are the subject of my hymn,
which they earned with their valor by defeating their enemies.

(67–80)

Under Doric law and the guidance of the king and his son, the
people may gain honor and live in "harmonious peace." The allusion
to music is surely meant to remind us of the hymn to the Lyre and the
peaceful rule of Zeus portrayed there. Having asked for concord among
the citizens and their kings, the poet then prays that the city may enjoy
immunity from foreign attack, and recalls Hieron's defeat of the Etruscan fleet at the Battle of Kyma in 474. He calls their act "aggression"
(*hybrin*, 72), and credits the victory with saving Greece (i.e., the Italian Greeks) from slavery. This ringing phrase "and delivered Greece
from grievous slavery" naturally leads into the praise of three other
crucial battles that saved Greece from foreign domination. They are
reported in a priamel. They are the Battle of Salamis (480), for which
the Athenians took credit; the Battle of Plataia (479), won by the
Spartans; and the Battle of Himera (480), won by Heiron's older brother Gelon in alliance with Theron of Akragas. The description of each
battle is one line longer than the preceding one, and although the poet
does not go so far as to say that the Battle of Himera was greater than
the others, it receives special emphasis by coming last, by having more
said about it, and by being won by one family, whose "valor" (*aretāi*,
80) earned them this hymn.

Once again the poet has reached a high point. He has reviewed the
great battles in east and west that have preserved the freedom of
Greece, and ended the fourth triad with the conquered enemies (*pole-
miōn*, 80) that recall Typhon as enemy (*polemios*, 15) of the gods. By
means of a very elaborate transition, the last triad turns to domestic
governance:

Strophe 5

If you tell the gist by combining the strands of many things
in brief, men are less apt to criticize, for nagging
tedium dulls keen expectation;
then too, citizens can be grieved in their secret hearts,
especially when they hear of another's success.

(81–84)

The poet ended his praise of "Deinomenes' sons" with the resounding lines on the Battle of Himera (80). He must relax the tone before proceeding to his next theme. Pindar often uses the first person in transitional passages, as he leaves one theme and prepares for the next. For example, at lines 42–45, he highlights the coming praise of Hieron by comparing himself with an athlete: "In my eagerness to praise that man, I hope not to throw, like an athlete. . . ." Here he addresses himself in the second person: "If you tell the gist. . . ." It is as if Pindar were letting us overhear his considerations as he composed his song. There are many such passages in the odes,[14] and they reveal the rhetorical and poetic principles that underlie his poems.

In this passage Pindar appeals to the principle of brevity, preferring to give the gist in summary form rather than providing a detailed elaboration. One implication is that he has much more to say about the success of "Deinomenes' sons," but intends to omit all the details. That way, he tells himself, "men are less apt to criticize." Pindar shows considerable sensitivity to the psychological limitations of his audience, and offers two reasons why they might prefer brevity: (1) tedium can result and make them unwilling to listen any longer, and (2) too much praise of one man can cause surreptitious resentment and envy in his fellow citizens.[15] In short, he suggests that his listeners may be growing weary of hearing all this praise, but that he could, if he wished, go on at much greater length.

On the other hand, if these principles of brevity and concern for the limitations of the audience are applied too rigorously, then there will be little incentive for noble action or fitting praise. Consequently, Pindar turns to Hieron with the counterproposition (85–86):

> But nevertheless, since it is better to be envied than pitied,
> do not forgo any noble things.

"But nevertheless" is a strong expression and always denotes in Pindar a forceful rejection of a previously expressed limitation. Pindar has just cited men's inclination to be envious of success as a reason for curtailing his praise, but that is no reason for Hieron to quit succeeding. Envy may be the price paid for success, but it is certainly preferable to being pitied for one's failure.[16] At this point, Pindar turns to exhortation, and the rest of the ode consists of advice to the king (and, of course, his son):

> Guide your people
> with a rudder of justice; forge your words
> on an anvil of truth.

Antistrophe 5

> Even a slight thing, you know, becomes an important matter,
> if it chances from you. Many things are in your control, but many
>   are the sure witnesses for good or ill.
> Abide in flourishing high spirits,
> and if you love always to be well spoken of,
>   do not trouble too much about the costs,
> but let out the sail, like a ship captain,
> to the wind. Do not be deceived,
>   my friend, by shameful gains,
>   for the posthumous acclaim of fame

Epode 5

> alone reveals the life of men who have died
> to writers and poets. The loving-minded excellence of Kroisos
>   does not perish,
> but that man of pitiless spirit, Phalaris, who burned others
> in his bronze bull, is overwhelmed by universal execration,
> and no lyres in banquet halls welcome him
> into gentle fellowship with boys' voices.
> Success takes first prize, and high esteem
>   comes second; but the man who can try for both
> and wins them, earns the highest crown.

> (86–100)

In the chapter of his *Rhetoric* dealing with epideictic oratory, Aristotle points out the ways in which praise and counsel are interrelated (1367b37 ff.):[17]

Praise and counsels have a common aspect; for what you might suggest in counselling becomes encomium by a change in the phrase. Accordingly, when we know what we ought to do and the qualities we ought to possess, we ought to make a change in the phrase and turn it, employing this knowledge as a suggestion. For instance, the statement that "one ought not to pride oneself on goods which are due to fortune, but on those which are due to oneself alone," when expressed in this way, has the force of a suggestion; but expressed thus, "he was proud, not of goods which were due to fortune, but of those which were due to himself alone," it becomes praise. Accordingly, if you desire to praise, look what you would suggest; if you desire to suggest, look what you would praise.

Likewise, Pindar's counsels (here and elsewhere) bear a close relationship to praise; as Aristotle points out, the real difference is in the phrasing: counsel is expressed as a command, "Be generous!" while praise is in the form of a statement, "He is generous." In his transition in lines 81–84, Pindar had shown concern that his praise might bore his listeners or arouse their envy. By couching his praise in counsel, he avoids both. The staccato phrasing quickens the pace, and the exhortative tone takes the servile edge off the praise. The poet becomes, for a moment, Hieron's peer, if not his superior; in line 92 he addresses him as "my friend" (ō phile).

The advice is basically (1) rule justly, (2) speak the truth, (3) be scrupulous with all in your care, and (4) be generous. By skillfully combining these principles of noble behavior and good government, Pindar has painted the picture of an ideal prince. He never says explicitly that Hieron "is" that ideal prince, but he suggests that he approximates it, for the present imperatives imply "keep on. . . ." And if Hieron and his son Deinomenes are wise enough to heed the poet's counsels, he holds out for them the possibility of poetic immortality. In fact, the poem itself awards it.

In the closing epode, Pindar gives two examples—one good and one evil—of fame after death. The first is that of Kroisos, the Lydian king who lived around 550 B.C.[18] His great wealth and munificence were legendary. Pindar calls his generosity "loving-minded excellence" (phil-ophrōn areta), and in those words sums up his message to Hieron: loving kindness and areta. In line 90 he reminds Hieron: "and if you love (phileis) always to be well spoken of, do not trouble too much about the costs." Forms of the word philos occur three times in the last eleven lines, and they convey the spirit of friendship that Pindar has for Hieron and that Hieron is exhorted to have for his people. Also, in line 60 Pindar had called his poem a "loving hymn" (philion hymnon) for Deinomenes. He is clearly depicting a community of mutual affection bound together by wise counsel and loving-minded areta.

Kroisos's "loving-minded excellence" is then contrasted with the negative example of Phalaris, the cruel tyrant of Akragas who was contemporary with Kroisos. He was notorious for roasting his victims in a great hollow bronze bull, so constructed that their screams would sound like the bellowing of the beast.[19] Instead of praise, he receives execration, and no lyres welcome him as the theme of songs sung by boys. And with the word "lyres" (*phorminges*), we are reminded of the poem's opening address to the "Golden Lyre" (*phorminx*) and of the power of music to soothe or to oppress, to praise or to censure, to inspire love or hatred. For Pindar, music and poetry are no mere aesthetic pastimes, but are active forces that combat evil and foster good throughout society and the cosmos.[20] The poem ends with a general reflection on the relationship of poetry and action. Success comes first, for *areta* must be realized in action, but the high esteem conferred by poetry comes next. When the two are in harmony, as action and contemplation (or practice and theory), then a man wins the highest crown: he will continue to live in fame, his "excellence . . . does not perish" (94). Pindar implies that Hieron aspires to that achievement.

After this close examination, it is time to back up and to put the whole poem together. In its largest sense, the ode is a hymn to order, whose basic principle "harmonious peace" (70) is embodied in the lyre, Apollo's "spokesman" and instrument of harmony that initiates and governs the dance and song. The effect of this music on those who are themselves in harmony with order is pleasurable calm. Its effect on those who are "without Zeus's love" (13), who are enemies of Zeus's order, is the opposite. Typhon is tormented by its sound, and sends up rivers of lava from his harsh imprisonment beneath Mt. Aitna.

On the national level, the Greeks who obey the sound of the lyre in their songs and dances also participate in the order of Zeus. And only recently they miraculously preserved that order from efforts in the east (Persians) and in the west (Carthaginians and Etruscans) to destroy their culture. On the level of the *polis* there is the founding of a new city, Aitna, under Doric laws and in the traditions that have made Hellas great. That founding is fittingly celebrated in an ode composed itself in Doric meter and dialect. And on the level of the individual, there are Hieron and his son Deinomenes, who, counterparts on earth of Zeus's order in the universe, must model their rule on the examples and precepts that Pindar provides throughout the poem, but especially in the last triad. Kroisos and Phalaris are telling examples of the proper and improper use of power and success; the emphasis on the latter makes the warning stronger, especially since he was a Sicilian. From what we know of the ruthless politics of western Greece, the abuse of power was all too common.

From beginning to end, the poem celebrates the power of music to make life pleasant and meaningful for those who join its fellowship. It provides forgetfulness of hardships and remembrance of *areta*. Those who defy its harmony suffer defeat and execration. On the divine level, Typhon lies imprisoned in painful frustration; on the national level, the Persians are defeated at Salamis and Plataia, the Carthaginians at Himera, and the aggression (*hybrin*, 72) of the Etruscans is stopped at Kyma; and on the individual level, Phalaris is excluded from the fellowship of his own nation. But Hieron, who has performed great Panhellenic service by twice rescuing Greek civilization from slavery, who even now is extending its boundaries by founding a new city, and who competes in the great national festivals, is immortalized in Pindar's song; like Kroisos before him, he can become a model for posterity to follow. It is hard to imagine another poem of one hundred lines that excels this one in its scope, seriousness, beauty, and ability to epitomize an entire civilization.[21]

Pythian 3. This ode defies precise classification. It mentions the fact that Hieron's horse Pherenikos was "once" (*pote*) victorious at the Pythian games, and probably for this reason it was grouped with the other two Pythian odes to Hieron. But since it does not commemorate a specific victory, it is impossible to determine its exact date. It had to have been composed before Hieron's death in 467 or 466, and its tone suggests that Hieron is possibly ailing or growing old, but there is no way of knowing just when, or for what occasion, it was composed.[22]

It stands in sharp contrast to *Pyth*. 1. While *Pyth*. 1 contains more direct allusions to historical events than any other ode, *Pyth*. 3 has none at all. *Pyth*. 1 contains no myth or extended narrative (only a description of Typhon and a brief reference to Philoktetes), but almost two thirds of *Pyth*. 3 is devoted to narratives and accounts of legendary characters: Cheiron, Koronis, Asklepios, Peleus, Kadmos, and Achilles, along with mention of Ischys, Harmonia, Thetis, Semele, Nestor, and Sarpedon. While *Pyth*. 1 is concerned with the public aspect of kingly rule, *Pyth*. 3 concerns personal conduct in the face of adversity. It is sometimes called a "poetic epistle." It is one of the greatest consolatory poems in all literature.

The poem is extraordinarily complex. Before going through it in detail, it will help to give an outline of the whole ode: contrary-to-fact wish: "If it were right . . . I would pray that Cheiron were still alive . . as he was when he once raised the hero Asklepios" (1–8); story of Koronis (9–37); birth, career, and death of Asklepios (38–58); gnomes (59–62); recapitulation of the contrary-to-fact condition: "Yes, if wise Cheiron were still living, and if my hymns could put a charm in his heart . . . ." (63–64); contrary-to-fact conclusion: "I would have persuaded him to provide a healer . . . and I would have come and brought him [Hieron] . . . golden health and a celebration" (65–76); Pindar's real prayer (77–79); consolatory advice to Hieron with examples of Peleus and Kadmos (80–115).

The first 76 lines express wishes that can never be fulfilled. Pindar cannot bring back Cheiron; he cannot bring Hieron health and success. These are utopian dreams. But in the midst of these vain hopes are the stories of two figures, Koronis and her son Asklepios, that illustrate the folly of human beings who are dissatisfied with their limitations. These narratives are presented in ring form in the opening strophe and antistrophe:

Strophe 1

If it were right for my tongue to utter that common prayer,
I would wish that Cheiron
were still alive, the departed son of Philyra
and wide-ruling offspring of Ouranos's son Kronos,
    and that he still ruled in Pelion's glades, that wild centaur
whose mind loved men. I would have him be as he was
when he once raised the hero Asklepios, gentle craftsman
    of remedies for pained bodies
and protector from diseases of all sorts.

Antistrophe 1

Before his mother, the daughter of Phlegyas the knight,
could bear him with the help of Eleithyia,
    goddess of childbirth, she was slain
by the golden arrows of Artemis
in her bedroom and went down to the house of Hades
    through Apollo's designs. The anger of Zeus's children
is no vain thing.

(1–12)

These lines are typical of ring-composition. The poet quickly outlines the principal figures to be treated in more detail shortly. We wait to hear what would happen if Cheiron really were alive, what Asklepios's career was like, and most of all, how a child could be born

from a dead mother. Our appetite is whetted to hear more about this
miracle; the poet will proceed in reverse order: Koronis, Asklepios,
and Cheiron:

> Yet she had made light of it
> through her mind's folly, and, unknown to her father,
>   accepted another husband,
> although she had previously lain with long-haired Phoibos;

Epode 1

and even though she was carrying the god's pure seed,
she could not wait for the wedding feast to come
nor for the ringing nuptial songs, with that childish banter
the bride's maiden friends love to sing
in evening songs. Oh, no!
She was in love with things far away—a common malady.
There is a very foolish type of person
who spurns what is at hand and peers into the distance,
seeking the impossible with hopes that never materialize.

Strophe 2

Yes, headstrong Koronis with the beautiful robes fell victim to
this great delusion: she slept in the bed
    of a stranger,
who came from Arkadia.
But she did not elude the Watcher, for although he was then presiding
    over his temple in sacrifice-receiving Pytho, Loxias heard of it,
and was convinced by the surest confidant,
his all-knowing mind,
    which knows no falsehoods, and is not deceived
by deeds or designs of god or man.

Antistrophe 2

And in this instance, when he realized her affair with the stranger
Ischys, son of Elatos, and her impious deceit,
    he sent his sister
raging with irresistible force
to Lakereia, for it was there by the banks of Lake Boibias
    that the maiden was living. Divinity turned
against her and slew her, while many neighbors
shared her fate and also perished. Fire that springs from one spark
onto a mountain can destroy a great forest.

(12–37)

The poet has completed one ring in the story of Koronis. In lines 9–10 he had said that "she was slain (*dameisa*) by the golden arrows of Artemis." We return to that point in lines 34–35, where "Divinity turned against her and slew (*edamassato*) her." Apollo and Artemis are angry in 11–12, and in 32–34 Apollo sends his sister "raging" to Lakereia. There is even a small ring in the middle. In line 25 Koronis "slept in the bed of a stranger," while in 31–32 Apollo realized "her affair with the stranger Ischys." The narrative technique is extremely artful; each time we return to a topic, it is with increased knowledge and accomplished with subtle variety.

A word is in order about Apollo and Artemis. Apollo was one of the most diverse gods in the Greek pantheon. He was a god of music (as in *Pyth.* 1), medicine (and plague), prophecy, archery, and even shepherding. Many stories were told of his intercourse with human women who bore him sons that brought his arts to mankind. Asklepios was one famous example, and Pindar tells of two others: Iamos the prophet (*Ol.* 6) and Aristaios the shepherd (*Pyth.* 9). Sometimes, the women would prove unworthy of the god's love and would suffer greatly. Kassandra in Aischylos's *Agamemnon* (see ll. 1202–12) is one such example. Apollo's weapon was the bow, and when he wished to destroy men, he shot his arrows of plague (the negative aspect of his power of medicine). Traditionally, Apollo would kill the men, while his twin sister, Artemis, would shoot the women. Thus, when he sends a plague to the entire region around Lake Boibias, it is Artemis who kills Koronis. Also, Koronis cannot hide from him (the "Watcher," 27) because as lord of his oracle at Delphi he knows all that man or god does or thinks.[23] He is no god to take lightly.

The portrayal of Koronis is exquisite, and little by little the poet lets us glimpse details of her character. She is foolish (13) and headstrong (24). She is too impatient to wait for the customary marriage rites (16–19). She has little regard for others, for she "made light of" Apollo's anger (12), disregards her friends' enjoyment of her wedding (17–19), and goes away "unknown to her father" (13). There is a sinister aspect as well. She elopes in secret, without telling her father, and in line 32 her action is called a "deceit." There is also the suggestion that the couple is hiding out and trying to "elude" (27) Apollo.

But the most important trait of Koronis is that "she was in love with things far away" (21–23):

> There is a very foolish type of person
> who spurns what is at hand and peers into the distance,
> seeking the impossible with hopes that never materialize.

Here is the moral center of this narrative about Koronis, and it sounds a leitmotiv for the entire poem. D. C. Young has shown how pervasive the theme of "the near and the far" is in this poem—and in Greek literature generally.[24] Twice it is emphasized that Koronis goes off with a "stranger" (25, 31), who comes all the way from Arkadia. Koronis is blessed with the favor of Apollo and could bear his child, but she is not satisfied with what she has and seeks what is yet beyond. Consequently she loses all, and even causes suffering for those who happen to be near (35–37):

> many neighbors
> shared her fate and also perished. Fire that springs from one spark
> onto a mountain can destroy a great forest.

Ironically, instead of living to bear a son that would be a doctor, she perishes in a plague. The gnome that ends this section contains a moral: one person's foolish misuse of divine gifts can cause widespread suffering; but it also introduces the important image of fire that runs throughout the poem and connotes destruction.[25]

Pindar has carefully constructed every aspect of the narrative about Koronis so as to establish the major themes and images for the rest of the poem. We still await the birth of Asklepios. The image of the fire continues:

Epode 2

> But when her relatives had placed the girl
> within the wall of the pyre and Hephaistos's flame burned
> fiercely around it, then Apollo spoke: "No longer
> can my soul bear to destroy my own son
> by a most pitiful death along with his mother's heavy suffering."
> Such were his words, and in one stride he came and snatched
> the child from the corpse, while the burning flame parted for him.
> He took him and gave him to Cheiron, the centaur from Magnesia,
> for instruction in healing men's distressing diseases.
>
> (38–46)

This epode completes yet another ring with its dramatic account of the miraculous rescue of Asklepios from his mother's corpse. The scene is painted with great care and the visual details are striking. The god's direct speech and his sudden epiphany mark this moment as a high point. His wrath with the mother does not extend to his son; the god still has pity on mankind's distress, and will give them another chance. The last lines (45–46), in which Cheiron takes the boy "for instruction in healing men's distressing diseases (*nosous*)" clearly echo lines 6–7: "Asklepios, gentle craftsman of remedies for pained bodies and protector from diseases (*nosōn*) of all sorts." Pindar follows with a catalog of the various diseases that Asklepios cured during his career—until he dared to cure the ultimate disease, death itself:

Strophe 3

When people came to him with cancerous sores
or with limbs wounded by grey bronze
or by a far-flung stone,
or with bodies wracked by summer fever
    or winter chill, he relieved them of their various ills
and restored them; some he tended with calming incantations,
to others he gave soothing potions or applied medicines
all over their bodies; still others he healed with surgery.

Antistrophe 3

But even wisdom can be the hireling of gain.
The sight of a lordly salary of gold in his hands
prompted even that hero to bring back a man
already taken to death. A swift cast from Zeus's hands
    took the breath from both men's breasts,
and the flash of lightning hurled doom upon them.
The mind of man must seek what is proper from the gods,
by knowing what is at our feet and what our human condition is.

Epode 3

Do not strive, my soul, for the life of the immortals,
but exhaust the valid means at your disposal.

                  (47–62)

Asklepios has inherited his father's medical skills but also his mother's foolish desires. Like his mother, he misused the blessings that Apollo had given him through his own selfish desires. Like her, he grasped for more, rather than being satisfied with what he already had. He, too, tries to get away with the impossible; he wants to bring back what is distant (the dead man). In his case there is no delay. Zeus immediately blasts both Asklepios and the revived man with his lightning; the image of fire is suggested again.

The narratives of Koronis and Asklepios are completed. They are
tragic stories and provide warnings. In the following four lines (59–
62) Pindar draws the moral with a gnome (59–60) and self-exhortation
(61–62). The gnome is essentially an elaboration of the two maxims
inscribed on Apollo's temple at Delphi: "know thyself" (*gnōthi seauton*)
and "nothing in excess."[26] We humans must seek what is "proper" from
the gods by knowing (*gnonta*) what is at our feet (i.e., the "near") and
the limitations of "our human condition." We must rely on the gods
for help, but in order to seek what is "proper" from them, we must
know what our resources and our limitations are. The poet then phrases
it slightly differently in an address to his own soul, two of the most
famous lines in Pindar: "Do not strive, my soul, for the life of the
immortals, but exhaust the valid means at your disposal." Paul Valéry
quoted them as the epigraph for his meditative poem on human existence, "Le Cimitière Marin." They capture the tension between man's
far-ranging hopes for godlike existence and the grim limitations of
death. They epitomize that Greek heroic outlook on life, where resig-
nation to the fact of death actually prompts the full use of one's powers.
This attitude finds its place in the Homeric world of the *Iliad*. For
example, at *Il.* 12.322–328, Sarpedon encourages his companion
Glaukos with the observation:

> Ah, my friend. If we two could escape from this battle
> and forevermore remain ageless and immortal,
> then I myself would not be fighting in the front ranks
> or urging you into the battle where men win glory.
> But as it is, spirits of death surround us
> in thousands, and no man can avoid or escape them;
> let us go, then, either to give away glory or to take it for ourselves.

Pelops expresses the same heroic sentiments at *Ol.* 1.81–85,[27] before
setting out to win glory. "The life of the immortals" here epitomizes
what is "distant"; to strive for it would be "seeking the impossible
with hopes that never materialize" (23).

Pindar finally returns to the opening of the poem, with its wish that
Cheiron were still alive. Now we find out what would have been the
consequences:

> Yes, if wise Cheiron were still living in his cave, and if
> my honey-sounding hymns could put a charm in his heart,

I would certainly have persuaded him to provide a healer
once again to cure the feverish illnesses of good men,
one called Asklepios or even Apollo.
And I would have come, cleaving the Ionian sea in a ship,
to the fountain of Arethusa and my Aitnaian host,

Strophe 4

who rules as king in Syracuse,
kind to his citizens, without envy for good men,
   a marvelous patron of foreign guests.
And if I could have come and brought him two joys,
golden health and a celebration
   to grace the Pythian crowns
that Pherenikos once won with his victory at Kirrha,
I swear that I would have outshone for him any heavenly star
when I arrived, crossing the deep sea.

                    (63–76)

The first two lines (63–64) recall the opening wish that Cheiron were still alive, and the rest of the passage consists of the logical conclusion (in grammatical terms, the "apodosis") of what would have resulted. Pindar would have persuaded Cheiron to provide another great healer. Then he would have gone to Syracuse. Lines 68 ("I would have come, cleaving the Ionian sea") and 76 ("when I arrived, crossing the deep sea") enclose a small ring that contains—at last!—mention of the poem's occasion. We are not told specifically that Hieron is ill, although the constant reference to disease implies it. But in a far more significant way, Hieron suffers from all mankind's disease: mortality. The "golden health" that Pindar would bring him is part of the vain wish of "that common prayer" (1). Pindar's great love for his patron has, as it were, gotten the best of him and made him indulge these impossible hopes. The prayer itself is vain, for it seeks to bring back someone (i.e., Cheiron) who is "departed," that is, distant and irretrievable. The very stories that Pindar tells—and, of course, his very reason for telling them—demonstrate the foolishness and futility of desiring what one cannot have and thereby losing the blessings one does have. In short, Pindar deliberately undercuts the grounds of any such prayer.

At this point the poet returns to reality and prays a legitimate prayer:

Antistrophe 4

But for my part, I wish to pray
to the Mother, whom maidens often hymn along with Pan
    at my door during the night,
for she is a venerable goddess.

                            (77–79)

This passage has caused a great deal of controversy and its meaning is far from clear. We know very little about the Mother Goddess (Magna Mater, Kybele, Rhea, or Demeter) and no completely convincing explanation of her presence or significance here has been offered.[28] But D. C. Young has pointed to one detail that is very important: she is celebrated "at my door." [29] In the context of this poem she represents the "near" and the feasible. The prayer to her thus represents the most Pindar can do for Hieron's health; the rest is up to the gods—and to Hieron himself, whom Pindar advises in the remainder of the poem:

Yet, Hieron, if you can understand the true point of sayings,
    you know the lesson older poets teach:
the immortals give men two evils for every good.
Now fools cannot bear them gracefully,
but good men can, by turning noble things outward.

                            (80–83)

The mention of "older poets" is precise and refers to the famous passage in book 24 of the *Iliad*, when Achilles consoles Priam for the loss of Hektor. At lines 527 ff., he tells Priam that there are two urns on the doorsill of Zeus, one of good and the other of evil. Some men receive portions from each urn and have a mixed lot; others just receive the evil. Pindar read the text more pessimistically (and the Greek is actually ambiguous enough to read it either way): there are two urns of evil and one urn of good. This allusion to the *Iliad* clearly marks the present poem as a consolation in the tradition of Achilles' speech to Priam.

The advice consists of a contrast between "fools" (*nēpioi*, a word from the epic and didactic traditions, used only here in the epinician odes), who do not accept their limitations, and the "good men" (*agathoi*), who display their noble achievements and blessings (*ta kala*). The point is basically the same as line 62: make the best use of what you have. Fragment 42 contains very similar advice, spoken (we are told) by Amphiaraos to his son: "One must show openly and to all the people one's portion of beautiful (*kalōn*) and pleasant things; but if men meet with painful evil from the gods, the proper thing is for them to hide it in darkness." Pindar now turns to Hieron's *kala*:

Epode 4

You have your portion of happiness,
for the ruler who guides his people is favored
by great destiny, if any man is. Yet an untroubled life
did not abide with Aiakos's son Peleus
nor with god-like Kadmos, although their happiness is considered
the greatest of any men, for they heard the singing of
the golden-crowned Muses on the mountain and in Thebes
of the seven gates, when Kadmos married ox-eyed Harmonia
and Peleus married Thetis, the glorious daughter of wise Nereus.

Strophe 5

The gods feasted with both of them
and they beheld the princely sons of Kronos
   on their golden thrones and received
their wedding gifts. By the grace of Zeus,
they recovered from their earlier hardships
   and their hearts were healed. But then in time,
the bitter suffering of three of Kadmos's daughters
bereft him of part of his joy, although at least Father Zeus
came to the longed-for bed of white-armed Semele.

Antistrophe 5

And Peleus's son, the only child immortal Thetis bore him
in Phthia, lost his life to an arrow in battle,
and as he was consumed by the fire,
he stirred the Greeks to lament.

(84–103)

In reminding Hieron of his portion of good fortune, epitomized by his rule over his people, the poet avoids mentioning any misfortunes he may have experienced; that would be "turning them outward." The lengthy account of the lives of Peleus and Kadmos provides what was to become a standard topic of consolation:[30] if greater men than you have died, then you can accept your own death. Peleus and Kadmos are the examples of human bliss at its greatest. They both married

goddesses, Kadmos in Thebes and Peleus on Mt. Pelion, and the gods
attended their weddings.[31] Pindar intertwines the description of their
happiness, but reserves the suffering of Peleus for the climactic position. Both men suffer through their children. Kadmos is the "Theban"
example of Pindar the Theban and exemplifies the "lesson older poets
teach" (81), for the suffering of three of his daughters is partially re-
deemed by his fourth daughter Semele's union with Zeus that produced
Dionysos. But Peleus fared even worse. He lost his only son Achilles
in the Trojan war. Once again we are reminded of Achilles' speech of
consolation to Priam in the *Iliad*, for immediately after telling about
the urns of good and evil, he continues (24.534–40):

> Even so, the gods gave glorious gifts to Peleus
> from his birth on, for he surpassed all men
> in happiness and wealth, and ruled over the Myrmidons;
> and although he was a mortal, the gods gave him a divine wife.
> But even on him god brought evil, since
> no strong sons were born in his hall,
> but he begat only one child, a short-lived one.

Pindar's consolation ends on a note of tragedy, with the lament of the
Greeks over Achilles' burning body. Once again fire provides a stern
reminder of mortality. For the last time, we move from a vision of
death to precepts. This time, however, Pindar addresses Hieron indirectly, and in the epode tactfully uses the first person, although it really
applies primarily to Hieron:

> If a mortal understands
>   the way of truth, he must make a success
> with what the gods give him. The breezes of the high-flying winds
> blow here and there. Men's happiness does not last long
> when it comes in full force.

Epode 5

> I shall be small in small times, great in great ones;
> I shall devote my thoughts to whatever divinity tends me,
> and serve him with the means at my disposal.
> And if god should grant me luxurious wealth,
> I hope that I might win lofty fame hereafter.
> Men still mention Nestor and Lykian Sarpedon, whom we know
> from those epic strains that wise craftsmen constructed.

Excellence endures in glorious songs
for a long time. But few achieve them easily.

(103–15)

Pindar's advice is consistent in the ode: take what the gods provide
and make a success of it. It is the "way of truth." The examples of
Peleus and Kadmos have also shown that man's happiness does not last
long, but is like the winds that change force and direction. After these
general reflections, the poet switches to the first person. The future
tense here is volitional and expresses his determination to adapt to
changing circumstances. These closing lines are full of echoes of previous words. Whatever divinity (*daimona*) tends (*ampheponta*) him, he
will serve him with the means at his disposal (*machanan*). We recall
that Koronis's divinity (*daimōn*) turned against her (34), that Asklepios
tended (*amphepōn*) his patients (51), and that Pindar tells his soul to
"exhaust the valid means at your disposal (*machanan*)" (62).

At line 110 he changes from the future indicative to the optative
mood. Whereas the future indicative expressed intention, the optative
mood indicates potentiality in the future. It is the mood of prayer and
hope. "And if god should grant me luxurious wealth, I hope that I
might win lofty fame hereafter." That wish sums up the positive message of the ode: the use of one's god-given resources to win fame. To
be "great in great times" and to "win lofty fame hereafter" are the same
two "prizes" we saw at the end of *Pyth.* 1: "Success takes first prize,
and high esteem comes second; but the man who can try for both, and
wins them, earns the highest crown."

In order to bolster the hope of Hieron's winning fame hereafter,
Pindar turns one last time to the *Iliad* for the examples of Nestor and
Sarpedon.[32] Nestor was the wise counsellor for the Greeks and Sarpedon
was a son of Zeus, who fought for the Trojans and was killed by Pa-
troklos. These two lived on in fame because of the epic verses that wise
"craftsmen" (*tektones*) constructed. The reference is clearly to Homer
and the epic poets, but the word "craftsmen" echoes the opening description of Askelpios as the "gentle craftsman (*tektona*) of remedies for
pained bodies" (6). Doctors and poets are both craftsmen; the one tends
the body, the other the spirit. Pindar's consolation concerns far more
than mere illness. Medicine cannot provide "immortal life" (61) or even
"golden health" (73), but poetry can provide a kind of immortality in
fame. The entire poem is about poetry as "medicine": no one can cure
Hieron of his mortality, but Pindar can make him live in memory as

Homer did for Nestor and Sarpedon. Poetry is the "medicine" for mortality; it is the ultimate consolation.[33]

"Excellence (*areta*) endures in glorious songs for a long time." It is fitting that the ode should conclude with that key term, for *areta* contains within itself the notion of the full use of one's powers and talents, the "means at our disposal." The last words of the poem add the sober reflection: "Few achieve them easily." Success in life (and in writing poetry) does not come easily and few are "distinguished for their *areta*" (*Nem.* 7.7). Hieron, it is implied, is one of those few. Pindar tactfully avoids comparing Hieron to Achilles, but does suggest that he might deserve to enter a select group of lesser Homeric figures such as Nestor and Sarpedon. That is, of course, if Pindar can do for him in his verses what the epic "craftsmen" did for them. The poem proves that he succeeded.

These close analyses are, admittedly, hard going, but there is no other way to convey an idea of the subtlety, scope, organization, and general movement of a Pindaric ode. At every point the poet is in complete control, and every minor detail fits into a complex whole. The poems were written to be appreciated in linear fashion from beginning to end, as we have done, for the audience (at least initially) heard them that way. But the complexity and sophistication of these works is such that close, repeated readings are necessary to perceive the relationship of the various elements. An ideal listener (like the ideal spectator at a Sophoklean or Shakespearean play) could conceivably have appreciated all the intricacies at one hearing, but these odes were composed to "endure for a long time," and that means to endure many rereadings. The attentive reader of Pindar is continually surprised by subtle nuances of expression, thought, and feeling that were overlooked in previous readings, and one never feels that he has exhausted the richness of even the shortest Pindaric ode.

But to offer such a detailed analysis of the remaining forty-three odes is obviously out of the question. The best we can do is survey the rest of the poems and selectively treat some of the highlights.

Olympian 1.   This is probably the best-known Pindaric ode. It may well have been the best-known lyric poem in antiquity. We have already noted that the early editor, Aristophanes of Byzantium, placed it at the head of the collection.[34] Its splendid opening, "Best is water . . ."[35] provides a good introduction to the grand sweep of his verse and his "imagery of the superlative."[36] Recent scholarship has revealed the ode's structural and thematic complexity.[37]

At its heart is Pindar's refashioning of the story of Pelops. Pindar recoils from those popular tales about the gods eating Pelops's flesh. On the contrary, when his father Tantalos gave a feast for the gods, Poseidon (who had been in love with Pelops) took him away to heaven. Subsequently, because of Tantalos's sins against the gods, the young Pelops was returned to the human realm. When he matured, he desired to win Hippodameia as his bride. But her cruel father, Oinomaos, challenged all her suitors to a chariot race, and when they lost, he killed them. At a high point in the ode, Pelops prays to his former lover, Poseidon, to help him win Hippodameia. The prayer vividly captures the heroic ideal (*Ol.* 1.75–85):

> If the loving gifts of Aphrodite gain any favor,
> Poseidon, come! restrain the bronze spear of Oinomaos
> and speed me in the swiftest of chariots
> to Elis, and give me strength to win.
> For he has killed thirteen suitors
> and delays the marriage
> of his daughter. A great risk captivates no man
>   who is a coward.
> But since men must die, why would anyone sit in darkness
> and stew a vain and nameless old age,
> without any noble deeds? No! this contest
> shall be mine; you grant the success I desire.

Of course, Hieron ran no personal risk by having his jockey compete in the Olympic horse race; we must not look for a one-to-one correspondence between the myth and the victor. What Pindar is portraying, however, is the original heroic spirit that informed this legendary first Olympic contest. The historical Olympic competitors also had to leave the security of home and risk defeat. It required tremendous effort, training, and courage to participate in the games; like the thirteen suitors, many lost and remained nameless. The Olympic games were no place for cowards. Even sending a horse or chariot required considerable expense and risky odds.

Pelops's prayer recalls Achilles' famous choice in *Iliad* 9.410–416 between a short life of action with undying fame or a long life at home without renown. It also recalls Sarpedon's speech to Glaukos quoted above by making mortality itself the stimulus to heroic action: "But since men must die. . . ."

After praising Hieron for his victory and for his high station as king, Pindar concludes the ode with a prayer (115–16):

> May you walk on high for the rest of your life, and may I
>   spend my time in company with
> victors, foremost in wisdom among Hellenes everywhere.

For Pindar, achievement and poetry depend on each other: song needs deeds to celebrate, and success needs song to make the *areta* last. This prayer is also a declaration of Pindar's poetic ambition: to be the foremost in wisdom (*sophiāi*) among Hellenes everywhere (*pantāi*). He aspires to be the Panhellenic poet of wisdom.

Pythian 2.   Of the four odes to Hieron, *Pyth.* 2 is the most mysterious. The ancient authorities were divided on whether it celebrated a victory in the Pythian games or in the Theban games, since all the poet says is that he is bringing from Thebes the announcement of Hieron's chariot victory. Consequently, it is impossible to date the ode precisely.

It has often been noted that all four odes to Hieron contain extensive portrayals of wrong conduct: Typhon in *Pyth.* 1, Koronis-Asklepios in *Pyth.* 3, Tantalos in *Ol.* 1 and Ixion in *Pyth.* 2. It is initially surprising to find so much attention paid to theft, adultery, murder, rape, venality, and ingratitude in public odes celebrating one of the most powerful rulers in the Greek world. As a result, many commentators have sensed an atmosphere of court intrigue and vicious poetic rivalries behind the poems, and especially behind *Pyth.* 2, where Pindar deals so extensively with ingratitude and slander. No doubt there were such intrigues (Sicilian politics were noted for their instability), and there was probably rivalry among poets vying for patronage. But alluding to such matters in a public ode on a ceremonial occasion would be in remarkably bad taste and would offend the very patron one was praising.

Instead, scholars have come to realize that Pindar never portrays just the bright side of life, but is always conscious of the dark side with its treachery, pain, and failure. From this awareness stems his frequent use of negative examples that act as "foil" to highlight by contrast the preciousness of success in a world so prone to vice. It is an aspect of his pessimism: "the immortals give men two evils for every good" (*Pyth.* 3.81). Praise and blame are opposite sides of the same coin, and Pindar is a master of both. Like the dark background of a Rembrandt, this negative foil makes the light shine forth with more intensity. Even on the level of diction, negative vocabulary and metaphors constantly operate to paint a richer picture of human existence, within which success stands out all the more remarkably. To take but one example, Pelops's description of the coward who "sits in darkness" and "stews a vain and nameless old age" highlights his own heroic choice of action in the public realm.

Pindar's portrayal of Ixion's fall in *Pyth.* 2 is a fascinating psychological study that shares many features with other examples of failure in the odes to Hieron. Ixion was generously given a carefree life in heaven among the gods, but he could not bear his continuous happiness. He went insane and conceived a desire for Hera, Zeus's wife. His aggressive lust drove him into delusion, and through a trick of Zeus, he made love to a cloud that he thought was Hera. He ended up in Hades, bound to a whirling wheel. A constant issue in Pindar's odes to Hieron is the proper use of happiness (*olbos*). Ixion could not "sustain" his *olbos* (*Pyth.* 2.26), Tantalos could not "digest" his (*Ol.* 1.55), and Koronis and Asklepios were not satisfied with theirs. Ixion went insane and lusted for Hera. Koronis provides a parallel case: she slighted Apollo's anger "through her mind's folly" and "was in love with" distant things. Ixion's aggression (*hybris*) led him to delusion (*auatan*). We recall the aggression of the Etruscans, which led to their suffering (*Pyth.* 1.72), and the "great delusion" (*auatan*) of headstrong Koronis (*Pyth.* 3.24), which led to hers. These odes analyze the progression from happiness to failure through lust (*erōs*), folly (*auata*), and overreaching (*hybris*).

We know from *Pyth.* 3.105–6 that "men's happiness does not last long when it comes in full force." Either the gods take it away (as in the case of Peleus and Kadmos) or men abuse it and consequently lose it. The examples of the latter have a particular relevance to Hieron. Of course, Pindar is not suggesting that Hieron is a Tantalos or Ixion; the point is precisely the opposite: Hieron is praised for the generous use of his power and wealth. The negative examples give the measure of Hieron's achievement, while at the same time they serve as admonishments: such happiness as Hieron's can go to one's head. The great power he possesses calls forth the great examples of its misuse.

In an elaborate transition halfway through the ode,[38] Pindar redirects the poem from the recounting of Ixion's failure to the immediate occasion, the praise of Hieron. This praise (57–67) is more lavish than that of any other ode: Pindar calls Hieron the wealthiest and most honored Greek ever, and extols him for his "boundless fame" won in battle. Fittingly, he concludes this praise by mentioning Hieron's "more mature counsels." The ode then ends with a long "rider" in which Pindar vigorously defends Hieron's sagacity and his own role as a forthright counsellor to the noble.[39]

Conclusion.   All four odes to Hieron display a remarkable combination of praise of the good, censure of the bad, illustrations of right and wrong conduct, exhortation, consolation, and admonition. All are united in their intention of immortalizing Hieron as a model for an enlightened ruler.[40] This is especially true of the three Pythian odes, which can be seen as early examples of "mirrors of princes" (*Fürstenspiegeln*).[41]

Chapter Five
Pairs of Odes to
Other Important Patrons

Olympians 2 and 3 to Theron of Akragas

We have noted that 476 was a very important year in Pindar's career. He composed five of the fourteen Olympian odes for victors in that year's games. We have already looked at *Ol.* 1 for Hieron, who won the single horse race. On the same occasion, another powerful Sicilian, Theron of Akragas, won the chariot victory.

Theron became tyrant of Akragas (modern Agrigento) on the south coast of Sicily in 488 and reigned until his death in 472 (or 471). He shared in Gelon's victory over the Carthaginians in 480 and initiated a building program that helped make Akragas one of the most beautiful Greek cities.

Olympian 2. *Ol.* 2 is one of Pindar's masterpieces. Whereas its companion ode, *Ol.* 3, is in dactylo-epitritic meter, *Ol.* 2 is composed of an iambic meter unique among the epinicians. It is by far the grander of the two odes to Theron, and the opening lines are among the most famous in Pindar: "Lyre-ruling hymns, / what god, what hero, and what man shall we celebrate?" Horace imitated them in his ode to Augustus (*Odes* 1.12.1–3):

> Quem virum aut heroa lyra vel acri
> tibia sumis celebrare, Clio?
> quem deum?

And Ezra Pound parodied them in *Hugh Selwyn Mauberley* 3.57–60:

> O bright Apollo
> τίν’ ἄνδρα, τίν ἥρωα, τίνα θεόν,
> What god, man, or hero
> Shall I place a tin wreath upon!

Pindar's scheme: "what god, what hero, and what man?" illustrates (in descending order) the three basic levels of his victory odes. The gods are primary; as Pindar says in *Pyth.* 1.41: "the gods provide all the means for human achievements (*aretais*)." The heroes provide the models of human *areta*. And the man, by his victory at Olympia (with all that it represents), has kept alive that heritage. There are also temporal aspects of these three levels. The gods represent all time (since they are immortal), but especially the future: they are constantly requested in the odes to provide future blessings. The heroes represent the past: their deeds, preserved in legend, provide paradigms of personal and social conduct. The man in each ode is the present embodiment of this divinely inspired *areta* in the heroic tradition. These three levels are present in every ode, and they give these poems their remarkable breadth of vision that embraces the universal and particular; the past, present, and future; and the divine and human.

In line 6, he calls Theron "the bulwark of Akragas."[1] Then he moves quickly on to praise Theron's ancestors for their hard toil in making their city "the eye (i.e., pride, cynosure) of Sicily," and for their wealth, grace, and inborn talents (*aretais*). The poet then prays to Zeus that he will preserve the land for their descendants. In these opening verses we see the successful Theron poised between a long past of great toil and an uncertain future that Zeus controls. The central portion of the poem elaborates on this temporal balance, and its overall structure reflects the movement from past to present to future. Here is an outline: gnomic reflections on the impossibility of changing what has happened in the past, whereas success brings forgetfulness of evil (15–22); examples of Kadmos's daughters (22–30); gnomic reflections on the uncertainty of human life (31–34); examples of Theron's Theban ancestors (35–45); the victories of Theron and his brother (46–51); gnomic reflections on success, wealth, and *areta* (51–56); a vision of the afterlife with punishment of sinners and rewards for the just (56–83).

It is obvious that gnomes articulate the parts of this progression. They provide the generalized reflections that are then illustrated with specific examples. The entire section dealing with the past (15–45) is divided into two parts. The first deals with the daughters of Kadmos (whose suffering was mentioned in *Pyth.* 3.96–99). They represent an older legendary time, whereas the next examples from the house of Oedipus are more recent, and, since Theron apparently traced his ancestry back to Thersandros, Oedipus's grandson, they facilitate the return to Theron in line 46. Two propositions dominate this entire section: (1) that human existence is subject to continual alternation of terrible suffering and great joy, and (2) that since the past cannot be changed, present happiness must redeem past suffering. The gnome at lines 15–22 sums up these themes:

> Whether deeds are done
> justly or unjustly, not even Time,
> the father of all, could undo their result.
> But they may be forgotten, if good fortune should come,
> for noble joys kill the pain
> and suppress its malignancy,
> whenever divine fate sends
> happiness towering upwards.

This view of life is characteristic of the pessimism of Pindar. Time is above justice; human life is entirely dependent upon the gods; humans constantly experience unpredictable alternations of great pain and joy. It is essentially the tragic view of life. It warns us to use to the fullest our present happiness.[2]

From this long meditation on the past, we come finally to the present occasion, and the essential information is briefly given: Theron has won the chariot race at Olympia and his brother (Xenokrates, celebrated in *Pyth.* 6 and *Isth.* 2) has won at Delphi and the Isthmos. We would expect to hear more in praise of these brothers, and it appears to be forthcoming as Pindar lauds "wealth adorned with virtues (*aretais*) . . . the truest light for man" (53–56), and adds, "and if a man has it and knows the future . . ." (56). But he never completes the if-clause. Instead, he begins his most famous digression on the "future" with a lengthy description of the afterlife. This digression has been one of the most discussed passages in his works;[3] its eschatological vision is unique in the victory odes, although some elements also appear in fragments 129–133 assigned to his *thrēnoi* (dirges). Here is the entire passage:

> If a man has it and knows the future,
> that the violent souls of those who die on earth
> immediately pay the penalty—since sins committed in this world
> where Zeus reigns are judged beneath the earth by one
> whose sentence is harsh and absolute.

Strophe 4

But forever with equal nights
and with equal days of sunshine, good men
receive an easier life, and they do not vex the earth
or water of the sea with the strength of their hands
to earn a paltry living. No, those who joyfully kept their oaths
spend a tearless existence with the gods they honored,
while the rest endure pain too terrible to behold.

Antistrophe 4

But those with the courage to have lived
three times in either realm while keeping their souls
free from all injustice, travel the road of Zeus
    to the Tower of Kronos, where ocean breezes
blow round the Isle of the Blessed.
Flowers of gold glisten there,
some from radiant trees on land, while the sea
    nurtures others; with these
they weave garlands for their wrists and crowns for their heads,

Epode 4

in obedience to the just decrees of Rhadamanthys,
the trusty companion of great father Kronos,
husband of Rhea who sits on the highest throne of all.
Peleus and Kadmos are numbered among them,
and Achilles, brought by his mother, after she persuaded
the heart of Zeus with her entreaties.

(56–80)

Three separate groups are defined in this passage: the unjust who
suffer pain, the good and pious who lead a "tearless existence," and
those who through three lives have kept their souls "free from all injustice." This ascending progression from torment to bliss is marked
by increasingly elaborate and precise descriptions. The punishments of
the evil souls are vaguely presented, and their judge is not even named.
Strophe 4 portrays in more detail the lot of the pious who have "joyfully kept their oaths." They enjoy a life of ease in an eternal "equinox"[4]
in the company of the gods they honored. In line 67 Pindar again
mentions the lot of the damned in order to complete the ring with the
beginning of the description and to close off this section with dark foil
before the climactic portrayal of the Isle of the Blessed in the anti-

strophe and epode. In contrast to the punishment of the wicked, which Pindar shrank from describing, and the lot of the pious, characterized mainly by the ills they lack (e.g., "tearless existence"), the description of the Isle of the Blessed is full and precise. Here we see the Tower of Kronos, the isle with its breezes and golden flowers on land and sea, and the heroes with garlands on their wrists and crowns on their heads. Specific people inhabit this realm, where Rhadamanthys (one of the traditional judges in the underworld) presides along with Kronos and Rhea (the parents of Zeus). The presence of these latter indicates that this realm partakes of the "golden age" before the reign of Zeus. Here also are the same three heroes who appeared in *Pyth.* 3: Peleus, Kadmos, and Achilles.

This depiction of the eschatological future in that other world where justice is immediate and absolute contrasts with the previous portrayal of the "past" (15–45) in this world, where time "could not undo" deeds regardless of their justice. The tragic view of life is completed by an eschatological theodicy.[5] Many have pointed out that speculations on the afterlife were particularly prominent in western Greece, especially among the Pythagoreans and Empedokles, a younger contemporary of Theron in Akragas. Perhaps Pindar is expressing Theron's own beliefs here. At any rate, this stunning passage is meant to inspire the noblest hopes in a man like Theron, who has wealth "and knows the future." We still wait to find out more about Theron.

After a brief catalog of Achilles' achievements at Troy (81–83), Pindar suddenly breaks off his account of the Isle of the Blessed with a lengthy transitional passage before returning to Theron.[6] In this famous passage he contrasts the man "who knows many things by nature," with those who have merely learned their art and "are loud and long-winded, like a pair of crows that vainly cry against the divine bird of Zeus." This is one of several places where Pindar proclaims the superiority of natural talent over mere learning.[7] From it derives the later designation of Pindar as the "Theban eagle."

Finally, in line 89, Pindar appears as a bowman and asks a question that rings back to the opening questions of the ode: "Come, my heart, and now aim the bow at the mark; who is the target of our famous arrows?" The target is Akragas, and the city is praised for having produced the most generous man of the century.[8] This is very high praise, but Pindar issues his oath to its truth, and concludes the ode by saying that Theron's "joys to others" are, like grains of sand, beyond number.

In conclusion, four ideas run through this very beautiful and complex ode: pain, joy, time, and justice. Putting them all together, we may say that Theron recognizes the past suffering and toil of his ancestors, with the result that he fully appreciates the present success he enjoys. He uses his wealth to provide joys to others, while living in the expectation that justice will ultimately be rewarded in a future judgment. It is implied that this vision of future bliss sustains Theron: indeed, without such a hope, why would anyone be so generous?

Olympian 3. This ode is a fitting complement to *Ol.* 2. Shorter and less brilliant, it was evidently composed for the occasion of *theoxenia,* celebratory feastings at which the patron gods are considered to be present as guests. The first words of the ode straightforwardly state its intentions: "to please the hospitality-loving sons of Tyndaros" (i.e., Kastor and Polydeukes), to praise Akragas, and to celebrate the Olympic victory of Theron.

At the heart of the ode is the myth of how Herakles brought the olive trees to Olympia, to be the "most beautiful memorial" (15) of the games. The narrative is a complex example of ring-composition, and Pindar introduces it in the same way that Homer introduces histories of significant objects. For example, at *Il.* 4.105, Pandaros takes out his bow, made from the horn of an ibex, "which once. . . ." Here it is the olive, "which once. . . ." The story tells how Herakles had once seen the olive tree in the far north in the land of the Hyperboreans on one of his labors. Later, after establishing the original Olympic site, he realized that the place was "naked" without trees (24). He remembered the marvelous trees he had seen and brought some to Olympia. There is a complex symbolism in this story involving the ideas of coolness and shade, memory, and the Hyperboreans. The reason for Herakles' bringing the olive tree was that the place seemed "naked" and "exposed to the sharp rays of the sun" (24). Something more was necessary to grace the contests and to provide relief from the heat. The implication is that without a memorial to crown effort, the toil in the hot sun would find no relief. The olive is called "shady" (18), and it comes from the country of the far north (Hyperborean means literally "beyond the north wind") which is described as "shady" (14) and "cold" (32). The olive, then, represents the relaxation and soothing effects of victory and its recognition after the hard toil in the sun. All this is reinforced by the portrayal of the Hyperboreans in *Pyth.* 10, where they are associated with poetry, music, and immortality. This story of the olive reveals its essential nature as the fitting recognition of victory.

After the story of the olive crown, Pindar rings with the beginning of the poem, as he announces that Herakles and the Tyndarids are joining the feast, and that Theron and his family enjoy such athletic success because they honor the Tyndarids more than anyone else does. He then ends the poem with an abbreviated version of the opening of *Ol.* 1:

> If water is best, and gold the most honored possession,
> now Theron by his virtues (*aretais*) has come to the limit
> and from his home has reached the Pillars of Herakles.
>
> (42–44)

Theron has reached the "Pillars of Herakles" (i.e., the Straits of Gibraltar), a frequent "image of the superlative" in Pindar that defines the limits of the known world, beyond which no one can go. The oblique reference to Herakles fittingly concludes this ode in which he plays such a major role.

Pythians 4 and 5 to Arkesilas of Kyrene

Kyrene was a prosperous city that commanded a fertile plain on the northeastern coast of what is now Libya. It was founded about 630 B.C. by Battos (also called Aristotle by Pindar) from the island of Thera, at the urging of the Delphic oracle. Apollo was particularly honored at Kyrene, where his Karneian festival was also celebrated. In *Pyth.* 9, the third ode for a victor from Kyrene, Pindar tells of Apollo's love for the nymph Kyrene and his installation of her as the guardian of the queen city of Libya.

Arkesilas IV was the eighth king in the dynasty begun by Battos. Although the Battids had seen their share of political troubles, their reign of nearly two centuries was remarkable, considering the instability of Greek politics. *Pyth.* 4 and 5 were composed on the occasion of his victory at Delphi in 462. At the end of *Pyth.* 5, Pindar prays that he will win the chariot race at Olympia, and indeed he did at the next Olympiad (460). Unfortunately, he was deposed sometime thereafter and his long dynasty came to an end.

Pythian 5. Unlike its spectacular companion ode, *Pyth.* 5 is a straightforward encomium of Arkesilas. Its opening proclaims its theme: Arkesilas is the wealthy king of a thriving city, and he uses his god-given wealth in accord with his own "pure excellence" (*aretāi*, 2).[9] The rest of the poem praises the king for his justice (14), his power

(15–16), his glorious ancestry (55–102), his wisdom (109–11), his courage (111–13), his devotion to poetry (114), and most of all his athletic interests (115–17).

But besides this praise of the king, Pindar devotes almost thirty lines to his charioteer, Karrhotos, by far the most extended tribute to a charioteer in the odes. The scholia tell us that he was Arkesilas's brother-in-law, but there is nothing in the ode to confirm it. Pindar rarely gives any details about the actual contest, but here the victory was especially spectacular, for we are told that "forty charioteers fell" (49–50), whereas Karrhotos won the race with his chariot unscathed through the twelve laps.[10] He even dedicated his equipment (presumably the chariot and its trappings) to the shrine at Delphi, where it took its place beside a statue from Krete.

Also prominent in the poem is the god Apollo, whose festival, the Karneia, provides the celebratory occasion of the ode, as does the feast for Kastor and Polydeukes in *Ol.* 3. The poet neatly links the two aspects of Apollo, who rules at Delphi where Arkesilas has won, and who is the patron god of the festival being celebrated in Kyrene. Then, in recounting the favor that Apollo bestowed on Battos, Pindar provides an aretalogy of the god (60–69) that indirectly represents Apollo's benefactions to the city. At 60 he is called "founding father" (*archagetas*), for it was through his oracle that Kyrene was colonized. Next comes Apollo's skill in medicine (63): Kyrene was famous for its physicians and for *silphion*, a medicinal plant that has not been identified. In line 65 Apollo's musical attributes are mentioned; the present poem and festival are certainly instances of Kyrene's devotion to Apollo's music. Then comes peaceful good government (66); given stormy times in Kyrene, this is as much a wish as a fact. Finally, the list culminates in Apollo's oracle (69),[11] the efficient cause of Kyrene's colonization under the Dorians.

Arkesilas, like Hieron, rules a city on the edge of the Greek world, and Pindar goes out of his way to show his genealogical and historical connections with the mainland. In fact, Pindar himself claims a personal connection with the founding clan of Kyrene, the sons of Aigeus, whom he calls "my own ancestors."[12] And in a fine descriptive passage (90–98), the poet mentions the great street along which the processions for Apollo proceeded—from the tomb of the founder Battos, past the tombs of the kings who succeeded him. These kings, Pindar surmises, share in this present victory of their descendant, Arkesilas. Yet even in Pindar's picture of a well-established ruler in a prospering city showered with the diverse gifts of its patron god Apollo, there is a reference to previous civil disturbance ("winter storm," 10). We shall meet a casualty of that discord in *Pyth.* 4, where Apollo's medicine and music are also essential to the well-being of Kyrene.

Pythian 4. *Pyth.* 5 is in Aeolic meter and is about the normal length of a full-scale ode. In contrast, *Pyth.* 4 is in dactylo-epitritic meter and its 299 lines make it almost three times as long as any other ode. It is the closest of the odes to epic poetry in its movement and its leisurely treatment of the heroic central narrative, the quest for the golden fleece by Jason and the Argonauts. Whereas *Pyth.* 5 contains sustained praise of Arkesilas and his dynasty, *Pyth.* 4 only mentions the king briefly at several points and does not dwell on his achievements. Indeed, if we did not possess *Pyth.* 5, we might conclude from *Pyth.* 4 that Pindar had little acquaintance with or interest in the king, and was only telling the story of Jason for its own sake. But as is apparent from an examination of other paired odes in which Pindar consciously treats different aspects of his theme, *Pyth.* 4 presupposes the lavish praise of its companion, *Pyth.* 5. Also, we shall discover that the story of Jason has a much closer connection with the king than is first apparent.

Besides its unusual length, another striking feature of the poem is the surprising "rider" of the last thirty-six lines, which is an appeal to the king to recall a young citizen living in exile in Thebes. We have seen "riders" in the odes to Hieron (the advice at the end of *Pyth.* 1 and the justifications at the end of *Pyth.* 2), but the one at the end of *Pyth.* 4 is unique in the epinician odes, for it is a dramatization of a political reconciliation. When the entire ode is seen in that light, then the story of Jason takes on added significance.

Before an analysis of specific portions, here is a sketch of the entire ode: intention to sing of Arkesilas and of Kyrene's founder Battos, who after seventeen generations fulfilled a prophecy of Medea spoken to the Argonauts (1–12); prophecy of Medea that links the quest for the golden fleece with the foundation of Kyrene through Euphamos, one of the crew (13–56); essential information about Arkesilas's victory and intention to sing of the expedition of the Argo (57–69); the return of Jason to Iolkos and meeting with Pelias (70–168); the mustering of the crew and successful recovery of the fleece from Kolchis (169–262); appeal to Arkesilas to recall Damophilos from exile (263–99).

The poem opens with an address to the Muse: "Today you must stand beside a dear man, the king of well-horsed Kyrene . . . ." The word "dear" (*philoi*) is, as we have seen in *Pyth*. 1, a very important word: right at the beginning of this ode it strikes a note of friendship between the poet and the king that has overtones of equality and freely given counsel.[13] Thus the opening prepares the reader for the end of the poem, when Pindar indeed assumes the role of a friendly counsellor.

Passing by the prophecy of Medea and the recovery of the golden fleece, we shall concentrate on two episodes: the meeting of Jason and Pelias and the final appeal on behalf of Damophilos. Pindar's account of Jason is a typical narrative about a hero,[14] who as a young man is exiled from his rightful patrimony, grows up in the wild, returns, undergoes amazing tests of endurance that are passed with magical or divine help, and finally ousts the usurper and regains his kingdom. Jason's older cousin, Pelias, usurped the throne of Iolkos when Jason was an infant. Jason was raised by Cheiron the centaur, and when he reached maturity he returned to reclaim his rightful rule. Meanwhile, Pelias had been warned by an oracle to beware a man who came to Iolkos wearing only one sandal, "whether a foreigner or a citizen" (78). Pindar's description of Jason is striking (78–83):

> And at last
> he came, a wondrous man with two spears,
>   dressed in clothing of both types:
> native Magnesian garb perfectly fitted
>   his glorious limbs,
> but over it a leopard skin protected him from
>   chilly showers;
> the splendid locks of his hair were uncut
> and rippled down the length of his back.

Jason is between two worlds. He is both a stranger and a citizen; he wears the clothing of his native Magnesia, but he also comes from the wild, with his leopard skin and long hair, for he has been brought up by Cheiron. Even his missing right sandal symbolizes his half-way position. In the following lines (87–92), we may gauge the power of his presence from the reactions of the citizens who first encounter him.[15]

When Pelias comes and sees the missing sandal, he knows that his adversary has arrived. The dialogue between the two masterfully reveals their characters. Pelias is wary and carefully contrives the destruction of his rival; Jason is a model of candor, reason, and self-control. After celebrating in epic style with his relatives, Jason goes to the palace to face Pelias. During this tense interview, Pindar says that "with a gentle voice, Jason distilled conciliating language and laid a foundation of wise words" (136–38). Jason allows Pelias to retain all the lands and livestock he presently possesses, so long as he himself can hold the kingship which is his by right. Pelias agrees, but insists that Jason first recover the golden fleece. A crew is mustered, the Argo sails, and with Medea's aid Jason succeeds in yoking the fire-breathing bulls of Aietes (169–246).

Then, having completed the episodes that are essential to his purpose, Pindar treats the remainder of the story in summary fashion (247–59), in order to complete the ring with the opening of the poem by bringing the lineage of Euphamos the Argonaut down to the founding of Kyrene by Arkesilas's ancestors (259–62):

> And from there Apollo gave your family
> the plain of Libya
> to make prosper by honoring the gods, and to rule
> the divine city of golden-throned Kyrene
> by devising policy based on right counsel.

This is, of course, a tribute to the mythical and historical pedigree of the house of Battos, but the final clause adds a note of warning, for Pindar is about to appeal to the king's good sense to recall Damophilos. Here again, as in the three Pythian odes to Hieron, the poet concludes with advice for the monarch (270–76):

> You are a most opportune doctor, and Paian Apollo
> honors your healing light.
> One must apply a gentle hand to tend
> a sore wound.
> Even weak men find it easy to disrupt a city,
> but putting it back on its feet is difficult indeed,
> unless a god suddenly guides its leaders.
> These blessings are unfolding for you.
> Dare to devote all your serious attention
> to the cause of happy Kyrene.

Then, Pindar praises the qualities of the young exile (281–87) and once again appeals to Arkesilas to recall him (287–93). Finally, he concludes the entire poem with these lines (293–99):

But he prays that when he has endured to the end
   his grievous disease,
he may some day see his home, that he may join
   the symposia at Apollo's fountain,
and often let his heart enjoy its youth; and taking up
the crafted lyre he may attain peace among the wise citizens,
  without harming anyone, nor suffering at the hands of his compatriots. ∘
Then, Arkesilas, he would tell
what a spring of immortal verses he found,
   when he was recently a guest at Thebes.

This is a remarkable end to an already remarkable poem. B. L. Gildersleeve astutely remarks: "The poem was a grand peace-offering, and the reconciliation had doubtless been quietly arranged in advance."[16] It is not certain just who commissioned the ode, Arkesilas or Damophilos, but the situation is fairly clear: Damophilos, a talented young man, has for some unspecified reason fallen from favor and he sues for forgiveness and restoration. The poet urges Arkesilas to take this opportunity to help his city.

We noted the pervasive presence of Apollo in *Pyth*. 5, and he is likewise much in evidence at the end of *Pyth*. 4. In each of the three quotations above, he appears with a different aspect of his powers. At 259, it is Apollo who has granted Libya and Kyrene to Arkesilas's family and who wishes them to rule "by devising policy based on right counsel." Here is Apollo, founder and protector of cities. At 270, Apollo appears as Paian ("Healer") and honors Arkesilas's "healing light." Finally, at 294, Damophilos hopes to join the symposia at "Apollo's fountain" in the center of Kyrene. Here is Apollo as god of the lyre and of celebratory poetry, the fitting figure to conclude this poem that celebrates the peaceful restoration of political order.

The theme of medicine runs through this last part.[17] Arkesilas is a "doctor" and Damophilos has been suffering from a "grievous disease." It is clear that the disease is a metaphor for civil strife, and that the injunction to "apply a gentle hand to tend a sore wound" (271) means that Arkesilas must use kindness to heal the city's political divisions. As in *Pyth*. 1, Apollo's lyre symbolizes the role of poetry in effecting "harmonious peace" (*hēsychian; Pyth*. 1.70). Here Damophilos hopes to take up the lyre and "attain peace (*hēsychiāi*) among the wise citizens" (296). The "spring of immortal verses" (299) that he would bring from Thebes includes, of course, the present poem, which, in performance, would turn his wish into reality.

Finally, we must return to the myth in order to determine its relevance to the whole ode. Many have attempted to equate the "mythical" characters with the "historical" persons by identifying, for example, Pelias with Arkesilas and Jason with Damophilos, but no one-to-one correspondence is satisfactory.[18] Yet, although the story is not strictly allegorical, it is, in a larger sense, paradigmatic. The return of Jason as a young man to his home after a period of political exile and his use of soft words and reason, along with his gallant deeds and service, are meant to be a model for Damophilos's own intentions. Pelias, the wicked usurper, cannot literally stand for Arkesilas, especially since Pindar stresses his family's rightful rule through eight generations, but he does provide a negative example of the greedy ruler who selfishly blocks reconciliation. Arkesilas is presented with behavior to avoid, and Pindar strongly suggests that he would be another Pelias if he did not accede to the spirit of the present occasion. The scholia tell us that Damophilos was a relative of Arkesilas's. We cannot be certain of that, nor is it really important, for Greek politics are full of dynastic struggles and political exiles, and Pindar is presenting in general terms a model for political concord.

Jason represents the heroic ideal: a man of soothing words, deference to his teacher Cheiron, kindness to family, of noble aspirations and courage, and above mere material concerns, as his conceding the possessions to Pelias amply demonstrates. In this carefully portrayed episode of the meeting of Jason and Pelias, Pindar depicts the model of the bad tyrant who attempts to hold on to his power without sharing it, and of the good ruler who is schooled in the precepts of Cheiron. Like the Pythian odes to Hieron, this ode is also a *Fürstenspiegel*.[19] Thus, on one level, the ode is a glorification of Kyrene and the dynasty of Battos, but on another it is a portrayal of the principles of good government that are necessary to keep it prospering. We receive the impression that heroic efforts were necessary to maintain peace in Kyrene; before long they were to fail and Arkesilas would fall.

Nemeans 1 and 9 to Chromios of Syracuse (and Aitna)

Pindar also wrote a pair of odes for Chromios, a distinguished general and statesman. He originally served under Hippokrates, tyrant of Gela, for whom he fought at the Battle of the Heloros River in 492 (*Nem.* 9.40). When Gelon, Hieron's older brother, succeeded Hippokrates in 491, Chromios served Gelon and married his sister. When Hieron became tyrant of Syracuse in 478, Chromios served as his general (probably in southern Italy and at the Battle of Kyma) and also as the governor of newly founded Aitna and guardian of Hieron's son Deinomenes.

We do not know when Chromios won the victories celebrated in these odes, but the poems were probably composed between 476 and 474. *Nem.* 1 was apparently written to Chromios as a Syracusan, but *Nem.* 9 mentions "newly founded Aitna" (2) and must therefore have been composed after 476/5. Although these complementary odes are both composed in dactylo-epitritic meter, *Nem.* 1 is triadic, whereas *Nem.* 9 is "monostrophic," that is, it consists of successive strophes (eleven in all) with no antistrophes and epodes.

Nemean 1.   This ode for Chromios's victory in the chariot race opens the book of Nemean odes. It contains surprisingly little specific information about Chromios. Most of the praise is indirect or stated in general terms. Thus, the picture emerges of a man who has divine excellences (9), is very generous to foreign guests (20–24), is strong (26), has foresight (27–28), and uses his wealth well (31–32). We are not told that he is a great general and one of the most powerful men in Syracuse, but we can infer that he is extraordinary, for the ode's second half recounts the career of Herakles from infancy to apotheosis and strongly suggests that Chromios has the qualities of that hero.

A regular feature of victory odes is praise of the homeland. A good example occurs in lines 13–18, where Pindar bids his Muse to praise Sicily, and his procedure is worth examining closely.

> Sow, then, some splendor on the island, which Zeus,
>   the master of Olympos,
> gave to Persephone and with a nod of his locks
>   assured her that he would exalt
> fertile Sicily to be the best of the fruitful earth
>   with her rich heights of cities;
> and Kronos's son gave her a people of armed horsemen
>   enamored of bronze-armored war
> and often crowned with the golden leaves
> of Olympic olives.

This passage begins with the gods: Zeus on Mt. Olympos and Persephone, a patron goddess of Sicily, who lives in the underworld. These two gods sketch, as it were, the limits of the world in terms of height and depth. Sicily is at first praised for her agricultural fertility and for her wealthy cities. Then, Zeus grants her a people who excel in horsemanship, both in war and in athletics. Many subtle maneuvers make this catalog interesting. There are several movements: (1) from gods (Zeus and Persephone) to men; (2) from agriculture (fertile soil) to civilization (rich cities); (3) from war to athletics; (4) from the past (Zeus's nod) to the present. Also, there is a continual narrowing of focus, from the vast panorama of the gods of sky and the underworld, to the fertile island that is "best of the fruitful earth," to the cities on her "rich heights," to her inhabitants, and even down to the leaves of olives. Obviously this last, climactic detail is appropriate for a victory in the chariot race, and the mention of "Olympic olives" neatly echoes the beginning of the passage where Zeus is "master of Olympos." Finally, there is the rich and complex language[20] that really does "sow splendor" on the island with its "imagery of the superlative." Even in the smallest touches Pindar's language holds one's interest. For example, he refers to Sicily's "rich heights of cities." We would normally expect the adjective "rich" to modify "cities" rather than "heights," but he has transferred it (the technical term is *hypallage*) to create an arresting and lively image that is both literal (cities built on the heights) and figurative (heights rich with cities).

After praising Chromios in lines 19–30, Pindar enunciates a general statement (gnome) about the proper use of wealth that leads directly into the myth of Herakles:

> I do not desire to keep great wealth
>   hidden away in my house,
> but to enjoy what I have and gain fame
>   by helping friends, for much-toiling men
> share common expectations. For my part, I gladly
>   cling to Herakles when the theme is lofty virtue,
> and tell the old tale . . .
>
>   (31–34)

This is all indirect praise of Chromios. The gnome expresses the general principles that underly Chromios's great success: he uses the resources ("wealth") at his disposal to succeed and to gain fame and friendship. It is a variation of the advice that Pindar constantly gave to Hieron: "If you love always to be well spoken of, do not trouble too much about the costs" (*Pyth.* 1.90); "Success takes first prize, and high esteem comes second" (*Pyth.* 1.99); "And if god should grant me luxurious wealth, I hope that I might win lofty fame hereafter" (*Pyth.* 3.110–11). Wealth (and that includes talents and resources of all kinds) is meant to be used for the common good; then it purchases enduring fame: "the loving-minded excellence of Kroisos does not perish" (*Pyth.* 1.94).

And as a reason for helping friends, he adds: "for much-toiling men share common expectations." Here is the dark background of suffering humanity whose common bond is ultimately death. Pindar often reminds his patrons of this shared humanity in order to encourage them to be generous and relieve some of the suffering of "much-toiling men."[21] The mention of "helping friends" and "much-toiling" naturally leads to the paradigmatic hero, Herakles, who spent his life toiling to help others. Herakles is the most important single hero in Pindar's odes, for he is the great benefactor who labored on behalf of mankind, who rid the world of inhuman monsters, and who was finally rewarded with apotheosis. In sum, he is the model for all who labor in the public realm for the common good. It was he who founded the Olympic games and is the ideal athlete; his labors were sculpted on the metopes of the temple of Zeus at Olympia. Finally, he shares two important traits with Pindar himself: he is a Theban and his career is Panhellenic.

Nem. 1 and 10 are the only odes that end with lengthy myths. In most of Pindar's odes, the narrative comes in the middle and the poet returns at the end for direct praise of the victor. By putting it at the end of the poem, Pindar gives the myth greater emphasis, and the two poems in which he does so contain especially impressive narratives. The myth of *Nem.* 1 tells of the entire career of Herakles, but typical of Pindar's procedure it concentrates on one event and then sketches in the rest. This event is the famous episode when as an infant Herakles strangled the two snakes sent by Hera to kill him and his twin brother Iphikles. We have already analyzed the masterly depiction of this "tableau."[22] It ends, characteristically,[23] by describing its effect on an onlooker, Herakles' father, Amphitryon (55–58):

> He stood there, stunned with wonder both painful
> and joyous, for he saw the extraordinary
> determination and power
> of his son.

This moment captures the intense emotion of this event, where terror gives way to joy as the father recognizes the prodigious powers of his divine son.

Pindar then switches from this interior, domestic scene to the public realm. The seer Teiresias is summoned and foretells the career of Herakles "to all the people." The prophecy consists of two major parts: the first summarizes the struggles that Herakles will have with various monsters, culminating in his assistance to the gods in their final battle against the Giants; the second describes the apotheosized state of the hero as he feasts in heaven with his wife Hebe (Youth).

The poem ends with this vision of "peace" (*hēsychian*, 70) and celebratory feasting. We recall that Chromios has prepared a feast to celebrate his victory (19–22); Pindar also mentions that the beginnings of Chromios's life were divinely inspired (8–9). Although Pindar never explicitly says so, he means us to see a parallel between Chromios's character and career and those of Herakles. Any listener familiar with Chromios's generalship on behalf of the Greeks against the Carthaginians and Etruscans would see the analogy, especially since Greeks in the fifth century constantly regarded the battle of the gods and giants (in which Herakles participated) as an analogue for their struggles against the barbarians.[24] The vision of eternal bliss that ends the ode, like the vision of the Isle of the Blessed in *Ol.* 2, is not meant literally to await Chromios (or Theron), but is paradigmatic for the rewards of noble toil, particularly the lasting fame that poetry confers.

Finally, in this ode Pindar is not concerned with presenting a list of Chromios's deeds, but with portraying his character. In fact, the only specific achievement mentioned is his chariot victory at Nemea. Instead, we must infer his greatness from Pindar's portrayal of Herakles—the ideal that Chromios takes as his model. Pindar's praise is all the more convincing for its indirection.

Nemean 9. This ode, also to Chromios, is not strictly a Nemean, for it celebrates his chariot victory in the Sikyonian games. It was obviously composed after 476/5, because it welcomes the Muses "to the newly-founded city of Aitna" (1–2). It shares many features with *Nem.* 1. For example, it begins by praising Chromios's lavish hospitality: "his wide-open gates are inadequate for all the guests" (2). Like *Nem.* 1, it ends with a feast, but unlike Herakles' feast in heaven, this is the actual feast of celebration in Chromios's home. More striking, however, are the differences. *Nem.* 1 ended with the myth, whereas this ode has the more usual *A-B-A* form, where *A* represents the specific occasion and *B* represents the myth. This structure is emphasized by elaborate "ringing" of the finale with the beginning: *kōmos* "festivity" (50), Apollo (53), Sikyon (53), and Muses (55).

This ode emphasizes the martial side of Chromios and mentions his

first great triumph at the Battle of the Heloros River, where in 492 he
fought for Hippokrates, tyrant of Gela, against the Syracusians, a battle that paved the way for Gelon's rise to power. If the allusion to
battles "on the neighboring sea" (43) refers to the Battle of Kyma,
which figured prominently in *Pyth*. 1, then the ode must be dated
after 474. A probable reason for Pindar's mentioning only the Battle
of the Heloros River by name and for vaguely alluding to the others is
tact. If he mentioned Himera or Kyma by name, then he might be
obligated to give full credit to Gelon and Hieron, who were the commanders in chief. At any rate, lines 34–43 leave little room for doubt
that Chromios was an extraordinary general, whether commanding infantry, cavalry, or the navy (34).

The myth also marks a sharp contrast with *Nem*. 1. The stirring
narrative of Herakles' career in *Nem*. 1 was clearly meant to provide a
positive parallel for Chromios's. The narrative in *Nem*. 9 is very different. After stating that the Sikyonian games were founded by Adrastos
(9), Pindar announces his intention to praise that hero. To the reader's
surprise, the narrative that follows does not concern a glorious victory
but rather a terrible defeat. It recounts the exile of Adrastos from Argos
and the subsequent expedition against Thebes (the famous "Seven
against Thebes"), when he alone of the seven chieftains was not killed.
The account ends with the horrible vision of "corpses fattening white
smoke" (23), as "seven funeral pyres feasted on the young men's bodies"
(24), and with the spectacular end of the seer Amphiaraos, who was
swallowed up by the earth as he fled. With his thunderbolt Zeus split
open the earth in front of his chariot and covered him lest he die a
coward's death. A gnome (27) completes the tale of utter defeat:
"When the gods send panics, even their sons flee."

Clearly this ill-omened, disastrous attack on Thebes is a negative
example of the sort we have seen in the odes to Hieron. Of crucial
importance is the role of Zeus in the story. He sent signs to stop them
from going on the campaign, but in their greed they disregarded them
and willfully went to their obvious doom (19–21). It was Zeus who
mercifully spared Amphiaraos from a shameful death. And it is to Zeus
that Pindar prays immediately following the myth in lines 28–33. His
prayer consists of two parts: that such warfare may long be avoided,
and that the citizens of Aitna may long enjoy good government and
public celebrations. And he adds: "they are horsemen there, and their
souls are above wealth" (32). The expression "souls above wealth" is a
compact way of saying that they use wealth to noble ends that glorify

the city. They maintain the heroic values that put fame (*doxan*, 34) above mere personal gain (*kerdei*, 33). One term for this attitude is the Homeric value of "honor" (*aidōs*, 33) and its concomitant sense of shame at being a failure. It is this sense of honor that has guided Chromios through all his military campaigns (34–43).

Thus, the character of the people of Aitna is summed up in their champion Chromios. The aggressive campaign of the seven against Thebes that ended in disaster is contrasted with the honorable action of Chromios, who fought like a Hektor at the Heloros River (39–42). The heroic past is no monolithic block of glorious deeds, but contains models for both good and bad; Pindar uses both aspects in this ode. On the one hand, Adrastos is praised for his civic achievements in instituting the games in Sikyon, but on the other hand, he led the ill-fated expedition against Thebes. We are meant to see the similarities between Adrastos and Chromios (horse racing, kingship, and generalship), but also the differences. Chromios has the same heroic spirit but has not used his talents for bad causes. His soul is above wealth. His battles are all honorable.

At lines 46–47 Pindar uses a gnome to praise Chromios's high achievement in familiar terms: "If along with many possessions a man wins glorious fame, his mortal feet can tread no further height." Then, after portraying the peaceful (*hēsychia*, 48) celebration of Chromios's victory with its wine and song, he makes a final prayer to Zeus (the fifth time he is mentioned in the poem) that his poem may surpass all others in celebrating Chromios's achievement (*aretan*, 54).

These two odes to Chromios are certainly not as impressive as the great odes to Hieron and Theron. After all, he is not really of the same stature. Nevertheless, he is praised for the same quality they are: the use of his talents, position, and wealth in generous service to his fellow men. He also has the same aspiration that they do: for his *areta* he desires fame that will outlive him.

Pythian 6 and *Isthmian* 2 to Xenokrates and His Son Thrasyboulos of Akragas

Xenokrates was Theron of Akragas's brother, who was mentioned in *Ol.* 2.49 as having won chariot victories at Delphi and the Isthmos. According to the scholiast, who gives Aristotle as his authority, he won his Pythian victory in 490, which would make it just days before the Athenian victory at Marathon. The second ode, *Isth.* 2, was written perhaps twenty years later (470) after Xenokrates and Theron were dead. Both odes are unusual for the fact that they celebrate Xenokrates' victories but are addressed to (and more concerned with) his son Thrasyboulos. Besides these poems, we also have a fragment of an *enkōmion* (fr. 124) for Thrasyboulos:

> Thrasyboulos, I am sending you this chariot of lovely songs
> for after dinner, that it might be a sweet incentive
> for your gathered companions, the wine of Dionysos,
> and the Athenian drinking cups.
> It is then that men's wearisome cares vanish from
> their breasts, and all of us alike sail on a sea
> of golden wealth to an illusory shore;
> then the pauper is rich, while the wealthy . . .
> . . . .
> . . . increase in their minds, smitten by the arrows of the vine.

It is regrettable that this quotation breaks off and that we do not have more of this kind of Pindar's poetry.[25]

Pythian 6. This monostrophic poem consisting of six short strophes purports to accompany a procession to the temple of Apollo at Delphi. The walkway that wound up the hill to the temple was lined with small buildings called treasuries in which cities like Athens, Sikyon, and Corinth housed precious dedications to the sanctuary. The poem opens with a sudden command for silence, "Listen!" as if the procession were about to begin. But as the poem proceeds, the actual treasuries are transformed into a metaphorical "treasury of hymns" (5–14).

> Here at hand in the golden valley of Apollo has been built
> for the fortunate Emmenidai and for Akragas on its river,
> yes, and for Xenokrates
> a Pythian victor's
> treasury of hymns,
> which neither an alien winter storm shall attack
> with its relentless army from thundering cloud,
> nor wind shall strike and carry it
> to the depths of the sea
> in a deluge of silt.

Implicit here is a contrast between physical monuments and songs with respect to their endurance. Pindar is fond of mentioning the superiority of song over statues in commemorating deeds (e.g., *Nem.* 5.1–5) and, as we shall see, he ends *Isth.* 2, the companion poem to Xenokrates and Thrasyboulos, with such an assertion. Although the topic was commonplace in antiquity, Pindar's lines were probably in mind when Horace wrote the famous ode that concludes his third book (*Odes* 3.30. 1–5):

> Exegi monumentum aere perennius
> regalique situ pyramidum altius,
> quod non imber edax, non Aquilo impotens
> possit diruere aut innumerabilis
> annorum series et fuga temporum.

> (I have completed a monument more lasting than bronze,
> and higher than the regal structure of the pyramids,
> which neither devouring rain nor violent north wind
> can demolish, nor the countless succession
> of years or the flight of ages.)

In the following lines Pindar continues the metaphor of the poem as a building and says that its "porch" announces the victory of Xenokrates with the chariot at Delphi, but then turns to Thrasyboulos and devotes the rest of the poem to praise of his filial devotion. Pindar says that Thrasyboulos exemplifies the precept that Cheiron the centaur once gave to Achilles:[26] "First of all the gods, honor Zeus the loud-voiced lord of thunder and lightning, but then never deprive your parents of similar respect as long as they may live." Then Pindar provides an heroic example of filial piety by telling how Nestor's son Antilochos died fighting to save his father. The little vignette gives a lively dramatization of the incident and is neatly set off by ring-composition.[27]

Pindar then completes the poem with direct praise of Thrasyboulos (44–54):

> Of today's sons, Thrasyboulos
> has come closest to the standard of filial devotion,
> and follows after his uncle in all manner of splendor.
> He manages his wealth with intelligence;
> he culls a youth without injustice or insolence,
> and enjoys wisdom in the haunts of the Pierian Muses.
> And to you, Poseidon, lord of horse racing,
> he comes with a mind you greatly favor.

Sweet is his spirit,
and when he joins his companions in symposia,
he surpasses the perforated labor of bees.

These verses sum up the ideal of noble youth. Thrasyboulos carries on
the family tradition of splendor that his father Xenokrates and uncle
Theron have set; he uses his wealth wisely; even though he is young,
he is just and modest. He enjoys serious poetry; he is an avid sports-
man; and, finally, he is delightful company at symposia. Yet once
again, the poem ends with a reference to the relaxing, joyous occasion
of a symposium. Included in this praise are the three "unwritten" laws
of Greek morality: honor the gods, honor parents, and honor guests
and strangers. The four "cardinal" virtues are also adumbrated: justice,
temperance, wisdom, and courage.[28]

This is a courtly poem with little tension; there are no dark shadows,
no negative examples or warnings; it is essentially an extended compliment. The ode begins with a reference to Aphrodite and is a kind
of "love poem," in a long tradition of such tributes to noble youths
that can be found on cups, in poems, and even in speeches.[29] Because
of the fulsome tribute to Thrasyboulos and the elaborate comparison
with Antilochos, who was a prominent contestant in the chariot race
depicted in *Iliad* 23, some commentators (ancient and modern) have
supposed that he actually drove his father's chariot in the race. It is
most unlikely that he did. In the one clear case where the victor did
drive his own chariot (*Isth.* 1), it is specifically stated that he did so.
The more likely conjecture is that Thrasyboulos oversaw the entry and
personally commissioned the ode for his father, thus winning Pindar's
praise for his filial piety. We do not have to suppose that he actually
risked his life to merit the compliment. We shall also never know if
this poem was actually sung at Delphi in a procession to the temple.
Its fiction begins in that setting, but it ends in a symposium, and its
intimate sophistication argues against its being a processional. The
scholia tell us that Simonides composed the epinician ode for Xenokrates on this occasion. Of that we cannot be certain, but this ode
would certainly be a fitting complement on a smaller, more personal
scale.

Isthmian 2.   This companion poem is considerably later than the
previous one; most commentators place its date around 470. It shares
several features with the earlier poem, including the fact that it is
addressed to Thrasyboulos, that it begins with Aphrodite and poetic

eros, and that it has an intimate tone, unlike that of the stately epinicians to Hieron and Theron. Once again, though, the contrasts are
even more striking. *Pyth.* 6 was monostrophic and Aeolic; *Isth.* 2 is
triadic and dactylo-epitritic. There is also much more tension in the
poem. Most important of all is the fact that Xenokrates is now dead.

The poem divides into three parts. The first (1–11) contrasts poetry
of the past and present, the second (12–42) praises the accomplishments of Xenokrates, and the third (43–48) is an exhortation to Thrasyboulos. Each part opens with a direct address to Thrasyboulos.

The first section of the poem is one of the most remarkable passages
in Pindar.[30] It begins with the poets of old who wrote spontaneous love
poetry whenever a beautiful boy took their fancy. That was, the poet
tells us, before the Muse became a greedy hireling and silver-faced
songs were sold by Terpsichora. But now the Muse quotes the words
of the Argive man who lost his possessions and his friends along with
them: "Money, money makes the man." In contrast to *Pyth.* 6 with its
bright, courtly atmosphere, *Isth.* 2 opens with a sense of loss and bitter
experience. Times are tough indeed, and the poem seems to pose the
question: can the optimistic, courtly view be sustained in hardship?
And what is the nature of the hardship? Many commentators have
speculated that it is the downfall of Xenokrates' family, the Emmeni-
dai, in Akragas. That is certainly possible, but perhaps the fact that
Xenokrates is dead suffices to cast a shadow of loss over the poem. In
this respect its tone resembles that of *Pyth.* 3 to Hieron: it too celebrates past victories and offers consolation.[31]

When the poet again addresses Thrasyboulos at line 12 with, "But
you are wise," the implication is that Thrasyboulos understands what
harsh reality is; he is a man of discernment. The following catalog
includes Xenokrates' victories at the Isthmos (the ostensible occasion
of the ode),[32] at Delphi (the subject of *Pyth.* 6), and at Athens. The
Olympic victory mentioned in lines 25–29 is actually that of Xenokrates' brother Theron in 476 (celebrated in *Ol.* 2 and 3), but it is
linked to his victory at Athens by the fact that Nikomachos was the
charioteer for both victories. Furthermore, the focus has widened to
include "the sons of Ainesidamos" (28). Although Thrasyboulos has no
victories of his own to boast, he too is included in line 30, when Pindar
praises the entire family for its victory celebrations and patronage of
poetry.

With the catalog of victories completed, Pindar turns in the last
triad to praise of Xenokrates' character. After saying that the way is

easy to bring praise to the homes of famous men, he uses a metaphor from athletics (35–37):

> May I make a long cast with the discus and throw the javelin
> as far as Xenokrates'
> sweet temperament surpassed
> other men's.

The reference here is to two events in the pentathlon, the discus and javelin throws. We saw a similar metaphorical expression at *Pyth.* 1.42–45, when Pindar was about to praise Hieron. Both passages indicate that the accomplishments of the victor are so extensive that the poet will have to exert himself to match them in his performance.[33]

Pindar then catalogs Xenokrates' virtues, all aspects of his "sweet temperament." He was (the past tense indicates that he is now dead) respectful to his fellow citizens, he raised horses in the Panhellenic fashion, and he joyfully celebrated all the feasts of the gods. And, climactically, his lavish entertainment (*xenian*, 39) never ceased and knew no bounds. With the exception of filial piety and youthful discretion, these are essentially the same qualities Pindar had praised in Thrasyboulos in *Pyth.* 6.

Having completed the praise of the father, Pindar turns in the concluding epode to Thrasyboulos with the injunction to keep alive his father's excellence and sends this message with one Nikasippos (43–48).

> Therefore, since envious hopes hang about
> men's minds,
> let him never keep silent his father's excellence
> nor these hymns, for I assure you
> that I did not fashion them to remain stationary.
> Impart these words to him, Nikasippos,
> whenever you visit my dear host.

We do not know who Nikasippos is; this is the only place he is ever mentioned. The vague reference to the "envious hopes" serves the same function here that the "envy" (*phthonos*) did in *Pyth.* 1.85, where Pindar advised Hieron to continue succeeding even though some citizens might be envious: "since it is better to be envied than pitied, do not forgo any noble things." In the face of men's natural inclination to belittle greatness, Thrasyboulos must strive not to let his father's excellence (*aretan*) be silenced. Nor are "these hymns" (i.e., this poem and probably the others Pindar has composed for Thrasyboulos) to fall silent, for the poet fashioned them to move, and not—like statues—to remain in one spot in silence. Once again Pindar contrasts the verbal poetic craft and the static plastic art. By stressing the sound and activity of his poems, Pindar is urging Thrasyboulos to keep active the spirit of his father's excellence as portrayed in his songs. As F. J. Nisetich points out, the expression "father's excellence" (*aretan . . . patrōian*) can also mean "inherited excellence."[34] Now that Xenokrates is dead his son must keep alive the family traditions of excellence that Pindar has laid before him in the poem. The sobering opening with its emphasis on hard times and the closing reference to envy indicate that it will not be easy. In *Pyth.* 6.45 Pindar had said that Thrasyboulos "has come closest to the standard of filial devotion" (*patrōian . . . stathman*). He is now exhorted to keep alive his dead father's *areta*; his filial devotion has a new dimension.

The closing words, "my dear host" (*xeinon*, 48), sum up the relationship of the poet and his patron and recall lines 39–42, where Xenokrates (whose name means "host-strength") was praised most of all for his hospitality (*xenian*). *Xenia*, the guest-host relationship of mutual service and obligation, is a cornerstone of the heroic ethic. This poem does not end with a cheerful symposium, but with a sober reaffirmation of two men's friendship. Times are more difficult than they were; greater effort is needed to continue the tradition. This poem both consoles and exhorts.

Chapter Six
Odes to Various Individuals and Cities

Victors from Aigina

We have eleven complete odes (and eight lines of a twelfth) to victors from the island of Aigina—almost one fourth of the odes. No other city comes close to having so many. Aigina lies about fifteen miles off the coast of Attica. It was a small but prosperous maritime polis that rivaled Athens during the first part of the fifth century, but was eventually defeated in 459 and became part of the Athenian empire. Aigina could not boast the courtly splendor and magnificence of a Syracuse, Akragas, Kyrene, or Corinth, but it was very proud of its Doric traditions and especially of its particular heroes, the "Sons of Aiakos." One or more of the Aiakids is prominently featured in every Aiginetan ode. These odes are *Ol.* 8; *Pyth.* 8; *Nem.* 3, 4, 5, 6, 7, 8; and *Isth.* 5, 6 and 8.

Since these odes contain so many allusions to exploits of the sons of Aiakos, a brief sketch of their lineage and history will facilitate reading the poems. Here is the family tree:

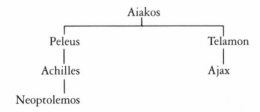

Aiakos, the patriarch, was the son of Zeus and the nymph Aigina, and was famous for his just rule over the island (*Nem.* 8.6–12). He joined the gods Apollo and Poseidon in building the walls of Troy (*Ol.* 8.31–52). Other traditions make him one of the judges in the underworld. His two sons were Telamon and Peleus. Because they killed their half-brother Phokos they had to flee from their native Aigina; Telamon went to the nearby island of Salamis, while Peleus went to Thessaly (*Nem.* 5.12–16). Telamon performed a number of exploits with the Theban heroes Herakles and Iolaos, including taking Troy for the first time from Laomedon (*Nem.* 3.37–38, 4.25–27; *Isth.* 5.35–38, 6.27–35). His son was Ajax (*Isth.* 6.36–56), the second-best fighter at Troy after Achilles. When the latter died, however, the Greeks voted to award Achilles' arms to Odysseus; in his anger Ajax committed suicide (*Nem.* 7.23–30, 8.23–34; *Isth.* 4.35–36).

The other side of the family was even more illustrious. When Peleus went into exile in Thessaly, he resisted the adulterous advances of his host's wife Hippolyta (*Nem.* 5.25–34)—the motif of "Potiphar's wife"—and was granted the sea nymph Thetis as his bride (*Nem.* 5.34–39; *Isth.* 8.26–47). To win her, he had to hold on to her as she changed into fierce forms (*Nem.* 4.62–65), but he succeeded and his marriage was celebrated by the gods themselves (*Nem.* 4.66–68; *Pyth.* 3.88–95).

Their son Achilles was raised by the centaur Cheiron (*Nem.* 3.43–55). He was the champion of the Greeks at Troy (as portrayed in the *Iliad*). Although he killed Hektor, Kyknos, and Memnon (*Isth* 5.39–42, 8.49–58), he died before Troy was taken. It was his son Neoptolemos who finally took Troy and killed Priam. After establishing his rule in Epiros (in northwestern Greece), Neoptolemos was stabbed to death at Delphi and was buried there (*Nem.* 4.51–53, 7.33–47; *Paian* 6.102–21).

As this sketch demonstrates, Pindar selects bits and pieces of this involved set of legends and works them into his odes at appropriate places. At times he merely alludes to them; at others he elaborates an episode into a narrative or a tableau.

Taken as a group, the Aiginetan odes present a fascinating picture of a relatively small Greek community that was devoted to athletics. With the exception of one Olympic victory (*Ol.* 8) and one Pythian victory (*Pyth.* 8)—both by boy victors[1]—the bulk of Aiginetan crowns were from the Nemean and Isthmian games. Many of the odes are to boy victors and all the victories are in gymnastic events: five in the pankration, four in wrestling, one in the penthathlon, and one in the diaulos (400-meter race). A small island like Aigina could not support horse breeding on the scale of Sicilian and mainland cities, but her athletes were powerful contenders, especially in the heavy gymnastic events.

In this highly concentrated athletic environment, particularly where so many young athletes excelled, two components stand out: inherited talent and training. Families and clans prided themselves on their numerous successes and secured the assistance of the best trainers for their young, aspiring boys. Every Aiginetan ode but two (*Nem.* 3, 7) mentions at least one major victory by a close relative of the victor. For example, in *Ol.* 8 to the boy Alkimedon, we are told that his brother Timosthenes had won at Nemea, that the present victory is the sixth major victory for the clan (the Blepsiadai), and that it is the thirtieth for his trainer Melesias of Athens. Pindar even pauses to praise Melesias for his own victories at Nemea and for his distinguished career of teaching.[2] Pindar was clearly fascinated by the interplay of destiny (*potmos*), inherited talent (*phya*), instruction (*didaskalia*), and practice (*meleta*).[3] On one level, *Ol.* 8 can be seen as an extended meditation on the interaction of these components: the same is true of many of the other Aiginetan odes.

The three odes to Pytheas and Phylakidas (*Nem.* 5; *Isth.* 5 and 6).   These three odes are to two brothers who came from a very athletic family. They were specialists in the pankration and their uncle Euthymenes had won at the Pythian games, while their grandfather Themistios had won at Epidauros. Pytheas was the older brother, whose victory in the boys' pankration is celebrated in *Nem.* 5. A large portion of an epinikion (13) by Bacchylides for this same occasion was recovered on the papyrus found in Egypt in 1896. Like Pindar's ode, it is dactylo-epitritic and devotes a major portion to the "sons of Aiakos." It also praises Pytheas's trainer Menander of Athens for his "man-helping training" (*meletan brotōphelea*, 191–92) and for his trainees' countless victories in Panhellenic games. Clearly this family spared no expense,[4] whether it came to hiring the best trainer available or the best choral poets of the generation to celebrate the boy's victory.

Isth. 6 celebrates the victory of Phylakidas (the younger brother) won at the Isthmos after Pytheas's Nemean victory. The central tableau depicts Herakles feasting with Telamon before the two heroes went off on their exploits. He stretches out his arms and prays that Telamon will have a son as powerful and brave as the lion whose skin he wears. At this point, Zeus sends an eagle as an omen, and Herakles declares that his prayer will be fulfilled and that the son's name will be Ajax (Aias) after the "eagle" (*aietos*). This myth is appropriate because it is about two of the sons of Aiakos, but also because it is about a noble father who has a noble son, and because Ajax (the sturdy, heavyweight fighter) is regularly an archetype for a pankratist. At the end of the ode Pindar praises the boys' father Lampon in terms that make clear one of the main reasons for their success: his complete devotion to athletics and his personal attention to his sons' training. Lampon, we are told (and we can almost hear the solicitous father), is fond of quoting a proverb of Hesiod to his sons: "practice makes perfect" (66–68).[5] Pindar goes on to call him a "whetstone" for athletes.[6]

Phylakidas went on to win another Isthmian crown, which occasioned *Isth.* 5, in many ways the most interesting of these three odes. It opens with a hymn to Theia (the "Divine One"), who is briefly mentioned by Hesiod (*Theogony*, 371–74) as the mother of the Sun, Moon, and Dawn:

Strophe 1

Mother of the Sun, Theia of many names,
because of you men value gold as mighty
above all other things.
And when ships contend
on the sea, and horses draw their chariots,
your honor, O Queen, makes them wondrous to behold
    in swiftly turning contests.

Antistrophe 1

And in athletic competitions, a man wins
desired fame, when many crowns wreathe his hair
after victory with his hands
or swift feet.

(1–10)

Typical of many opening hymns, it is in the form of a priamel. The terms of the foil are gold, ships, and chariots;[7] the climactic term (emphasized by its position at the start of the antistrophe) is athletic victory. Each of these terms has a concomitant value: gold is "mighty," ships and chariots are "wondrous," and athletic victory wins "desired fame." Sketched here are the most valuable, wonderful, and desired things in life; they are all comprehended under the power of the goddess Theia, who bestows honor on all aspects of life (hence she is called "of many names"). Here as well is the dominating image of "light" that we saw in the opening priamel of *Ol.* 1.[8] But in a way, Theia is even beyond light, for she is the originating principle of light itself.

H. Fränkel has shown how close Pindar comes here to Plato's idea of
"the Good" that gives value to all things in the universe, and is the
cause of light in the visible world (*Republic* 7.517B–C).[9]

At the end of this ode Pindar makes one of his few direct references
to current historical events by praising the role of Aiginetan sailors at
the Battle of Salamis (48–50):

> And now as well, Ajax's city of Salamis could bear witness
>   to their prowess in war, when their sailors saved it
> during the devastating storm of Zeus
> with its hailstorm of death for countless men.

Although the Athenians (and in particular Themistokles) rightly
claimed overall credit for engineering the victory at Salamis, Herodotos
(*Histories* 8.93, 122) tells us that the Aiginetans won the prize of valor
in the actual battle.[10] Scholars have frequently pointed out that as a
Theban Pindar is in a potentially embarrassing position, since his city
did not participate in the Battle of Salamis and actually fought on the
side of the Persians at the Battle of Plataia. But we must remember
that Pindar is foremost a Panhellenic poet, and here as well as in *Isth.*
8 (also to an Aiginetan victor) Pindar only expresses relief and praise
for these glorious victories that rid Hellas of the "rock of Tantalos," as
he calls the Persian threat in *Isth.* 8.10.

In sum, these three odes to a family of athletes from the small island
of Aigina not only celebrate particular victories, but also incorporate
legend, history, and even metaphysics. They portray the ideals that
guide this family—and Hellas—and ultimately all men who are under
Theia's light.

Nemean 7 to Sogenes of Aigina.   This ode is one of the most
intriguing and puzzling in the collection. The train of thought and
tone have proved so difficult to grasp that the noted Pindaric scholar
B. L. Gildersleeve labeled this poem "the touchstone of Pindaric criticism." Many scholars have sensed a defensive tone throughout the ode,
and since antiquity there has been the view that Pindar is apologizing
to the Aiginetans for the way he treated the death of their hero Neoptolemos in an earlier paian. Since the recovery of that poem—*Paian*
6—in 1906, this view has gained credence, but it is by no means
unquestioned.[11] For one thing, what Pindar says about Neoptolemos
in the paian is by no means derogatory, and the fact that it differs
somewhat from the version in *Nem.* 7 is not surprising for Pindar, who

frequently adjusts myths from one ode to another. What is extraordinary is that such a complex ode should have been composed for a boy victor.

In spite of uncertainty about the overall meaning of the ode, it contains many passages of note. We have already had occasion to look at the opening hymn to Eleithyia, goddess of childbirth.[12] She embodies both the similarities and differences of men. On the one hand, she represents the common ground of existence, for without her we would never see day or night nor mature to youth. Here birth (and later in the poem death) makes us alike. On the other hand, she represents the different destiny that constrains each person from his birth. And out of this summary sketch of man's different limitations, Sogenes is singled out as the beneficiary of both of Eleithyia's aspects: "By your grace Sogenes is famed in song, because he was distinguished for his excellence (*aretāi*) among pentathletes" (7–8). What "distinguishes" Sogenes is the realization (*areta*) of the potential that was his from birth.

In two places in the ode Pindar discusses the role of poetry in highly metaphorical terms. The first is at lines 11–16:

> If a man's action meets with success, he casts a honey-minded
> cause into the Muses' streams, for mighty deeds
> remain in great darkness when they lack hymns.
> We know of a mirror for noble deeds in only one fashion,
> if, by the grace of shining-crowned Mnemosyna,
> one finds a recompense for labors in poetry's famous songs.

This passage is an elaborate meditation on the relationship of action and song. When men's efforts ("action," "deeds," "labors") meet with "success," they provide "a honey-minded cause" (i.e., theme, motivation) for the Muses. Pindar first supports his assertion negatively: without hymns those feats remain in the great darkness of oblivion;[13] then positively: by the grace of Mnemosyna (goddess of memory, the mother of the Muses) the deeds are remembered in famous songs. Pindar offers three different metaphors to portray the nature and efficacy of poetry. First, it is called the "Muses' streams." Flowing water is a frequent metaphor for poetry, suggesting its steady movement, and perhaps its abundance, brightness, and nourishing qualities. Pindar frequently refers to his poems as "drinks" or "toasts." Another metaphor compares poetry to a "mirror" that reflects or imitates the deeds. And, finally, poetry is a "recompense" for labors; it is owed them and it keeps them

from sinking into obscurity. Noble deeds constitute a "cause" (elsewhere Pindar uses the metaphor of a "debt") that is sweet to the mind;
the Muses are glad to sing of success. Successful toil is thus rewarded
with famous songs (elsewhere Pindar also uses the metaphor of "salary"
or "wage"). The relationship is reciprocal: the song needs the "cause"
(theme) for its flowing verses, while the deeds merit the song with its
power to preserve them in memory. Action, success, brightness, memory, reward, and fame: these elements occur continually in Pindar's
poetry and point to the basic principles of epinician poetry.

Later in the poem, Pindar uses a striking metaphor to express the
rich and intricate complexity of his epinician poetry (77–79):

> Weaving crowns is easy work. Strike up the lyre. The Muse,
> you know, binds together gold and white ivory with
> the lily flower of coral which she has taken from under
>   the dew of the sea.

The metaphor is drawn from the craft of sculpture or jewelry-making
and emphasizes the poem as a richly wrought, precious article compounded of different but beautiful elements. The passage aptly describes an ornament meant to adorn the victor. In *Nem.* 3, another ode
to an Aiginetan, Pindar also refers to poetry as a mixture of elements,
but with an entirely different metaphor (76–79):

> I am sending you
> this mixture of honey and white milk
> topped with blended foam, a drink of song
> accompanied by the flutes' Aiolian breath.

Here, instead of a crown, the offering is a "drink" of song composed
of blended elements to celebrate the victory. The metaphorical expression emphasizes the sweetness and nourishing qualities of song.

Although other Aiginetan odes deserve fuller treatment than can be
given here,[14] it must suffice to treat the highlights of two odes to boy
victors from Aigina, *Nem.* 6 and *Pyth.* 8.

Nemean 6.   In the hymn to Eleithyia at the beginning of *Nem.*
7 we noted that Pindar was concerned with the similarities and differences among men. In the opening of *Nem.* 6 he similarly treats the
relationship between the gods and men:

> There is one race of men, another of gods; but from one mother
> we both draw our breath. Yet a completely different allotment

of power separates us: we are nothing, whereas
   the bronze heaven remains
a secure abode forever. Nevertheless, we do to an extent
resemble the immortals in the greatness of our minds or bodies,
although we do not know by day or in the night what sort of course
destiny has marked for us to run.

(1–7)

The ode opens with the differences: men and gods are of distinct races. But, they are similar in the fact that they both descend from one mother. In mythological terms, that mother is Gaia (Earth), who begat Kronos, Zeus's father, but in a larger sense both gods and men are compounded of elements from this cosmos: the Greek gods were "cosmic" gods who were material and very much a part of this world. Having established a common origin for both races, the poet turns to the greatest difference, their respective power (*dynamis*). Men are "nothing," whereas the gods are immortal. And yet, in spite of our impermanence, we do resemble the gods "in the greatness of our minds or bodies" (the Greek gods were in human form). But (and this is the last critical difference), man does not know the future and must live in uncertainty on a daily basis. Once again day and night symbolize man's "ephemeral" nature.[15] Divinity and nothingness: these are the poles of man's condition that underlie Pindar's odes. *Memento mori* (remember that you must die) is the warning behind all of Pindar's praise: "Do not seek to become Zeus. . . mortal things befit mortals" (*Isth.* 5.14–16). One should enjoy success, but by remembering that nothing human is permanent.

Pythian 8. Perhaps the most famous expression of Pindar's "pessimism" is found in the last triad of *Pyth.* 8 to Aristomenes of Aigina, who won the boys' wrestling at Delphi. Like so many of these young Aiginetans, he comes from a distinguished family of athletes; his maternal uncle Theognetos won the boys' wrestling at Olympia in 476.[16] A quotation at lines 44–45 sums up Pindar's reflections on inherited talent: "It is by nature that noble determination shines forth from fathers to sons." But at the end of the poem, Pindar's thoughts turn to the four boys whom Aristomenes defeated at Delphi (83–87):

> But they were not awarded such a glad
> homecoming at Delphi,
>   nor when they returned to their mothers did sweet laughter
> arouse joy all around; they shrink down alleyways to avoid
> their enemies, bitten by defeat.

Then, after reflections on how short-lived man's joy is, Pindar concludes with these reflections on the human condition (95–97):

> Creatures of a day! What is a person? What is he not?
> Man is the dream of a shadow. But whenever god-given brightness
>   comes,
> a shining light rests upon men and honey-sweet is their life.

Men are creatures of a day, "ephemeral" (*epameroi* in the poem's dialect).
We cannot know from day to day who we are, or if we will even continue to exist. Pindar's bold metaphor for the insubstantiality of human
existence is truly memorable: "Man is the dream of a shadow" (*skias
onar anthrōpos*). As one scholiast puts it, the expression depicts man as
"weaker than weak." Either dream or shadow would alone imply darkness and tenuousness, but their combination multiplies the effect.

Once again, human achievement is described as light that derives
from the gods. Whenever we receive that "god-given brightness" (*aigla
diosdotos*) then existence is illuminated with a "shining light" (*lampron
phengos*) and our life becomes "honey-sweet" (*meilichos*). The word *aigla*
implies the brightness of a gleam or flash that characterizes the sudden
realization of godlike qualities in man. In contrast, *phengos* implies the
steady brightness of a lamp or beacon, and characterizes the lasting
effects of achievement on the rest of one's lifetime. As Pindar says at
Ol. 1.97–99, "for the rest of his life, the victor enjoys a honey-sweet
(*melitoessan*) calm as far as games can give it."[17] Achievement casts a
light over all one's life; the dark nothingness disappears.

One scholiast says that some commentators criticize Pindar here "because in his enkomion he laments human life." Death, defeat, sorrow,
pain, suffering, transience, more evil than good, many defeated for one
victor—all this emphasis on the dark side of human existence could,
for one of lesser faith, verge on cynicism. But in Pindar it serves to
make even more brilliant the rare examples that emerge from this darkness, when life is illuminated by the favor (*charis*) of the gods, and a
man's efforts issue in success. He thus wins honor and praise, and perhaps is fortunate enough to leave behind his fame (*kleos*) preserved in
statues or poems.[18]

Conclusion to the Aiginetan odes.   In sum, the Aiginetan odes
portray a community that is dedicated to the heroic ideal: "I am delighted that the whole city strives for noble things," Pindar says of
Aigina at *Nem.* 5.46–47. Again and again she is praised for her hos-

pitality (*xenia*) to other Greeks, for her Doric traditions, and for her particular heroes, the sons of Aiakos. The eight lines that survive of *Isth.* 9 fittingly summarize Aigina's qualities:

> Famous is the story of Aiakos, and famous too is Aigina,
> renowned for her navy. By the will of the gods
> the Doric army of Hyllos and Aigimios
> came and founded her,
> and her citizens dwell in obedience to their rule.
> They do not violate right nor justice due to strangers,
> but in achievement (*aretan*) they are like dolphins in the sea,
> and are wise stewards of the Muses and of athletic contests.
>
> $$(1-8)$$

It is not by accident that this tribute ends with poetry and athletics. Pindar portrayed Hieron, Theron, and Arkesilas as model rulers; Aigina was his ideal *polis*.

Victors from Thebes

Pindar composed five odes for victors from his home town: *Pyth.* 11 and *Isth.* 1, 3, 4, and 7. They celebrate victories in chariot racing, pankration, and stadion. Since there is no certainty about the dates of any of them, we shall treat them in their order in the collection.

Pythian 11. *Pyth.* 11 celebrates the victory of Thrasydaios of Thebes in the boys' stadion. Until recently, the poem was much misunderstood and criticized because its myth seemed entirely inappropriate.[19] The noted German scholar Wilamowitz called it "one of Pindar's most obscure poems" and the ancient scholiasts were clearly puzzled as well. One obvious reason for confusion is the fact that the myth in the poem serves as a negative example. As we saw in the case of *Nem.* 9 with its story of Adrastos's defeat, Pindar occasionally uses a narrative to establish a contrast with the person being praised. Such is the case here. And since the poem contains a number of procedures that have baffled readers (both ancient and modern), it is important to examine it in some detail.

First of all, the introduction of the myth is remarkably abrupt. After an invocation to the Theban goddesses (1–12), Pindar announces Thrasydaios's victory in Delphi, "in the rich fields of Pylades, the host of Spartan Orestes, whom . . ." (15–17). The relative pronoun "whom" suddenly plunges us into the story of Agamemnon's death at the hands of Klytaimestra. This narrative has been aptly called a "little Oresteia" after Aischylos's great trilogy. It is told in ring-composition and, as usual, the end echoes the beginning: Pylades and Strophios are "hosts" for Orestes (16, 34) and Klytaimestra kills Agamemnon and Kassandra by stealth (19–22, 31–34). But in the middle occurs a very interesting deliberation on the motivation for the queen's pitiless deeds (22–25). Pindar wonders whether she was angry because of Agamemnon's sacrifice of their daughter Iphigeneia or whether her adultery with Aigisthos got the better of her. Pindar does not directly answer his question (any more than Aischylos does), but there is no doubt that the emphasis, as usual, falls on the second choice, especially in light of the observations that follow (25–30):

> This sin [adultery] is the most hateful
> in young wives and impossible to conceal
> because of others' tongues,
> since townsmen are scandalmongers.
> Then, too, prosperity sustains a matching envy,
> whereas the noise of a lowly man goes unnoticed.

These gnomes reflect on the relationship of power and envy. Pindar makes many of the same points at *Pyth*. 1.84–88, when he warns Hieron about the propensity of citizens for envying success and reminds him: "Even a slight thing, you know, becomes an important matter, if it chances from you. Many things are in your control, but many are the sure witnesses for good or ill." The slightest act of a person in high position is a public concern, whereas blatant actions of unimportant people go unnoticed. The higher the prosperity and power, the more envy it is exposed to. Thus, Klytaimestra's adultery with Aigisthos has become the talk of the town.

After these reflections on power and scandal, Pindar quickly returns to those dreadful events: the murder of Agamemnon and Kassandra. The myth ends with the return of Orestes, who "killed his mother and laid Aigisthos in gore" (37). The tale ends, literally, "in gore." One cannot help but wonder what all this has to do with a boy runner from Thebes! It is easy to see why Pindar gained a reputation for erratic genius and willful disregard for his subject. Even an ancient scholiast makes the following judgment: "Pindar began with an excellent enkomion, but what follows [i.e., the myth] is a completely irrelevant digression." What is more, Pindar seems to admit that he has gone astray in the following notorious verses (38–45):

> Truly, my friends, I got confused where the road forked,
> although I was on the straight road before; or did some wind
>   throw me off course
> like a small boat at sea?
> Muse, since you have contracted to hire out
> your silver voice, you are obligated to keep it moving
>   from subject to subject,
> either now to his father, a Pythian victor,
> or to Thrasydaios,
> for their glorious celebration is ablaze.

A transitional passage of this kind is very confusing for modern readers, who are not used to the sudden appearance of the poet in an ode, seemingly confessing that he has gone astray. Yet this procedure occurs several times in Pindar and is quite conventional in classical literature.[20] The point is invariably the same: "I appear to have been carried away by this topic; now it is time to get back to the main theme." Its function is, as Pindar says, "to move from subject to subject." It makes a clean break between one topic (usually treated at some length) and another, more relevant one. It is startling, and it is meant to startle; but it is a sophisticated procedure—the poet is not to be taken literally as an incompetent craftsman.

This passage combines three metaphors portraying poetic composition: traveling on a road, sailing on the sea, and meeting the terms of a business contract. All three indicate purposeful activity with a destination to reach or an obligation to fulfill. The poem must get somewhere; it has obligations. It has often embarrassed modern readers that Pindar should refer so openly to the fact that his poem is "hired out." We tend to be very squeamish about patronage and poetry that is written on commission,[21] but Pindar was more open about it. Not that he went begging in his poems (as some commentators have charged), but he constantly reminds himself (and us) that there is a real person to praise, and the "contract" can be invoked at any time to recall the poet to his obligated theme. Pindar uses this metaphor of the "debt" of song so often that it has come to be called the *chreos*-motif ("debt-motif"). Here the metaphor of poetic obligation is used to recall the poet from his treatment of the mythical past to the present celebration (note "now" in line 43), which is the motivating cause of the poem.

In short, Pindar actually means to suggest here that he has gotten "off course"; he is openly calling attention to the fact that the myth of Orestes appears to be entirely irrelevant. And in fact it is—at least at this point in the poem. By calling attention to the discrepancy, Pindar forces us to be alert for connections in the rest of the poem. Only when we have completed it can we judge whether or not the "digression" is ultimately relevant.

After praising the family for its athletic victories (46–50), Pindar makes a number of gnomic statements in the first person (50–58), and concludes with the examples of Iolaos and Kastor and Polydeukes (59–64). These last two passages are particularly important for providing the links between the myth and the family of Thrasydaios. Unfortunately, the text is incurably corrupt in line 56 (one of the few such places in the epinicians), but the overall sense of the passage is clear:

> May I desire noble things from the gods,
> and seek what is possible at my age.
> For I find that the prosperity of the middle estate flourishes
> longer in a city, and I censure the condition of tyrannies.
> I strive for achievements (*aretais*) that others share; it
>   wards off envy.
>
> (50–54)

The following three lines can be interpreted in a number of ways, but it is certain that the poet ends by praising the person who, at death, "leaves to his dearest offspring the greatest of possessions, the grace of good repute" (57–58). These gnomes recommend a certain way of life, the "middle estate," in which a man desires noble things that are "possible" for him and strives for achievements in which others share. He thus lives without being subject to envy (because his achievements are for the common good), and when he dies he bequeaths fame to his descendants. Here at last is the connection with the myth, and especially with its central gnomic passage, where Pindar was concerned with "scandalmongering" citizens (28) and with the "envy" (*phthonon*, 29) that prosperity (*olbos*, 29) sustains. Klytaimestra's adultery and private intrigues bring her infamy. Instead of inheriting a fair estate, Orestes comes from Delphi to a dishonored house. In contrast, Pindar recommends a life that strives for common interests, one in "the middle," whose prosperity (*olböi*, 53) is more lasting and avoids envious people (*phthoneroi*, 54). The result is fame after death, one of the "noble" goals of life.

The relevance of the myth is perfectly clear. In one way, Pindar really was "off course," for the story he tells is totally inappropriate to the present occasion. But that is precisely the point; it portrays the opposite extreme. Orestes returned from Delphi to a dead father and a shameful situation; Thrasydaios returned from Delphi to a father who was himself a Pythian victor, and to a city celebrating his victory in which they all share. Thrasydaios and his father are obviously not powerful men in the city, but they have "desired noble things" within their capabilities and achieved a lasting possession, good repute.

Perhaps because the myth illustrates the negative side, Pindar devotes the final epode to positive examples (59–64):

> This grace of good repute sends abroad the fame
> of Iolaos, son of Iphikles,
> in song, and of valiant Kastor,
> and yours, king Polydeukes, as you sons of the gods
> spend one day in your homes at Therapnai,
> and on the next dwell in Olympos.

Iolaos was the nephew of Herakles and his faithful squire; Kastor and Polydeukes were devoted brothers who alternated days in Hades and on Olympos.[22] They were all famous athletes and exemplify that noble striving for "achievements that others share." They are the models for Thrasydaios and his family. The house of Atreus in the myth is a home torn by hatred, adultery, and murder; it is subjected to the envy and slander of the citizens. Orestes inherited a curse and dissension; Thraydaios inherited the fame of his father's Pythian victory and matched it. The goddesses of Thebes were invoked at the beginning of the ode to praise and bring grace (*charin*, 12) to Thebes. Praise and grace are the rewards for those who live moderately and promote the common cause. It is no accident that the poem ends with fame (*euōnymon*, 58), grace (*charin*, 58), and song (*hymnēton*, 61). The last word Olympos is a reminder of the immortality that song bestows.

Isthmian 1. *Isth.* 1 celebrates the chariot victory of Herodotos of Thebes. Pindar begins the ode with a bit of "personal fiction." He says that he is going to set aside work on a paian to Apollo for presentation at Keos in order to write the present ode for a native son. After all, he says, "what is dearer to good men than their own beloved parents?" Pindar is not really discussing his personal life here, but rather turning his own Panhellenic talents toward a theme of particular interest and thereby fulfilling his filial duty (a virtue praised in *Pyth.* 6 and *Isth.* 2). This opening is a good example of Pindar's charming sophistication.

The ode has been thoroughly explicated in E. L. Bundy's monograph.[23] For our purposes, there are several points to note. First, Pindar tells us that Herodotos drove the chariot himself (15) and that this victory is the culmination of numerous victories in minor games. In this ode Pindar also presents positive and negative models of behavior. Lines 16–32 are a hymn to Iolaos and Kastor, who represent, as in *Pyth.* 11 above, the ideal athletes whose deeds redound to the glory of their native cities, Thebes and Sparta. In fact, Pindar explicitly says that he intends to "join" (*enharmoxai*, 16) Herodotos to his hymn for Kastor and Iolaos, a fitting description of his mingling the heroic past with the present achievement.

In contrast to *Pyth.* 11 with the negative myth and the positive examples at the end, this poem has the positive hymn and ends with a negative example. After cataloging Herodotos's victories (52–63) and praying that he will be inspired by the present victory and its celebration to go on to win at the Pythian and Olympic games (64–67), Pindar ends the poem with this observation (67–68):

> If a man keeps his wealth hidden at home
> and attacks others with laughter, he does not consider that he
> will pay up his soul to Hades—without fame.

This sketch portrays the precise opposite of Herodotos, a man who openly spends his wealth (and that includes his talent) to bring honor to his city and earn fame that will outlast his death. Thus Pindar defines the generous, heroic spirit of his addressee by depicting his opposite, the miser, who keeps everything hidden away for himself, who derides the very people he should be generous to, who "pays up" his soul to death (a grim comment on the miser's economics), and leaves no fame to survive him. He regards wealth as an end, and dies with nothing to show for it; Herodotos sees wealth as a means to winning posthumous fame.[24] Herodotos looks beyond death; the miser does not even consider its existence.

Isthmians 3 and 4.   These two odes to Melissos of Thebes create a problem for editors. Of the two major manuscripts, one treats them as separate poems, while the other gives them as one poem. The problem is that they are in the same meter. We have many other examples of two poems for one individual, but this is the only case where the meter is identical; in all other cases, Pindar goes out of his way to make them different. There are arguments for treating them as separate odes or as one continuous poem, but I find the evidence considerably in favor of separating them. The scholia treat them as two poems; the authority of the one manuscript that combines them is undercut by the fact that it also combines *Isth.* 2 and 3; they treat different victories; joining them creates an awkward transition; and, finally, they can stand on their own as independent poems.[25] If it were not for the meter, no one would have considered combining them. And yet many editors do combine them, and for that reason *Isth.* 5–8 are sometimes reduced by one number, making seven Isthmian odes instead of eight and reducing the total number of odes from 45 to 44.

Isth. 3 consists of only one triad. Although it makes a vague reference to an Isthmian victory, it really emphasizes a chariot victory at Nemea, and praises both sides of Melissos's family for their devotion to chariot racing. On its own, this poem would more appropriately belong among the Nemean odes. In many ways, it is an encapsulation of the themes that find fuller expression in its sister ode of four triads, *Isth.* 4. This latter ode celebrates Melissos's victory in the pankration at the Isthmos. Since it does not mention any chariot victory, a reasonable assumption is that after *Isth.* 4 was composed, Melissos went on to win a chariot victory at Nemea. Pindar broke with his usual practice of using a different meter for the shorter ode, and for convenience early editors placed it with the longer ode.

The two odes stress a common theme: the tension between permanence and instability. On the one hand is the abiding nature of the gods ("But the sons of the gods are invulnerable" [*Isth.* 3.18b]) and of man's "inborn excellence" (*aretan symphyton* [*Isth.* 3.13–14]); on the other is the impermanence of individual fortune ("As the days roll on, a lifetime brings many diverse changes" [*Isth.* 3.18–18b]). We have already seen this theme in other poems (e.g., *Ol.* 2; *Pyth.* 5, 8), and here Pindar uses a remarkable variety of metaphors drawn from nature to express the ups and downs of fortune. One metaphor is drawn from plants: "flourishing" (*Isth.* 3.6, 4.4) and "blooming" (*Isth.* 4.18b); another from images of dark (*Isth.* 4.18, 36) and light (*Isth.* 4.23, 42–43); another from shifting winds (*Isth.* 4.5); another from seasonal and weather changes (*Isth.* 4.18–18b); another from alternating days (*Isth.* 3.18). These and similar metaphors abound in all the odes to create a background of uncertainty and darkness periodically illuminated by success. In this ode the family of Melissos provides a good example. Long recognized at Thebes for its devotion to horse breeding and its prowess in war and athletics, it had its share of disappointment and sorrow. It could not seem to win a victory in Panhellenic games (*Isth.*

4.28–29) and, far worse, in a single day it lost four men in the "snow-storm" of war (*Isth*. 4.17–17b). But the ancient fame does still survive, and Melissos's victory has "awakened" it and brought light where there was darkness. In the long run, the family tradition endured; it had merely "fallen asleep" (*Isth*. 4.23).

Although much more could be said about these odes, one unusual detail deserves comment. Pindar rarely mentions a particular physical attribute of an athlete, but in the case of Melissos he does. He was evidently small and did not look much like a pankratist, but because of his determination and skill he was a giant-killer. Pindar compares him to "short" Herakles, who wrestled with the giant Antaios and finally defeated him by lifting him off the ground, thereby depriving him of the strength he derived from his mother Earth. This allusion to the Theban hero Herakles is particularly appropriate in this ode to a Theban, and the poem fittingly ends in joyous celebration.

Isthmian 7. *Isth*. 7 is for Strepsiades of Thebes, victor in the pankration. It opens with a hymnal priamel, as the poet addresses The-ba, the city's tutelary deity, with a series of questions (1–3):

> Which of your former native glories,
> O blessed Theba, most delighted
> your heart? Was it when . . .?

The list that follows surveys the past achievements of Thebes. Its order is essentially historical and its direction is the same as the opening of *Ol*. 2: god, hero, and man. First mentioned is Dionysos, who was (in some accounts) born at Thebes and hence her "native" god. Then come the heroes of war (Herakles and Iolaos) and of counsel (Teiresias the blind seer). The list concludes with two famous campaigns, the "Seven against Thebes," and the taking of Amyklai, when the Theban clan of the Aigeidai (to which Pindar may have belonged) helped the Spartans capture this important city.

Pindar's question is purely rhetorical; no answer is given. Instead, he uses the fact that these were all "former" glories to reflect on the role of poetry in keeping alive the tradition (16–19):

> But ancient splendor
> sleeps; and mortals forget
> what does not attain wisdom's choicest pinnacle
> by being yoked to glorious streams of verses.

The "splendor" (*charis*, which can also be translated "charm," "grace," "joy") of those olden glories becomes dormant through time, and they are forgotten if no one revives them in song (as, of course, Pindar is doing at the present time). The old needs the new in order to be remembered. At this point the poet can introduce "Strepsiades too" (21), who continues, as it were, this ledger of fame into the present. Theba can now celebrate (*kōmaze*, 20) her newest representative of "native glory." This priamel is one of the most impressive in Pindar's epinicians. It illustrates how his inclusive vision can embrace the old and the new, divine and human, and legendary and historical.

But after receiving a mere three lines of praise for his own achievement (21–23), Strepsiades shares his moment of glory with his maternal uncle of the same name, who was killed in battle, fighting in the front ranks for his homeland. Suddenly the mood changes from joy to sorrow; Strepsiades' victory not only revives joyful glories, but also consoles for sad ones. The poet's comment, as a fellow Theban, is painfully touching: "I endured inexpressible grief" (37). But now is the time for celebration, and the poet turns to a meditation on the future (40–50) that culminates in the prayer that Apollo might grant Strepsiades a Pythian crown.[26] Past glories, present achievement, hopes for yet further achievement—the poem moves steadily through time, sketching Thebes' native tradition and projecting it into the near future.

Selected Odes

Olympian 13 to Xenophon of Corinth. *Ol.* 13 is the only ode to a Corinthian; it contains grand praise for the athlete, his clan, and the city. It opens with the striking colon that consists of one triple compound adjective: "thrice-olympic-victorious." But after arousing our curiosity, Pindar moves immediately to praise of "prosperous" Corinth; we shall have to wait before hearing more about this family with three Olympic crowns.[27]

First, Corinth is praised for her three resident goddesses, the Horai ("Seasons"). They are the daughters of Themis ("Right") and are Eunomia ("Good Government"), Dika ("Justice"), and Eirena ("Peace"). These goddesses in turn ward off Hybris ("Aggression") and her son Koros ("Excess," "Satiety"). Pindar here depicts ethical principles in terms of genealogy: Themis and her daughters are a part of the natural order (as "Seasons" the Horai still maintain a close association with nature), whereas Hybris and her son represent violence and excess that are unnatural. In abstract terms, the splendid wealth of Corinth rests on adherence to natural principles of good government, justice, and civil order, which help the city avert immoderate aggrandizement.

Next Pindar proceeds to the achievements of the people themselves. He singles out their distinction in athletics and their inventiveness (14–17). We shall soon see these two come together in the person of the victor, but first he enumerates three Corinthian inventions: the dithyramb, the bridle, and the pediment of a temple. This is indeed high praise for the city, and Pindar concludes it with a prayer that Zeus will continue to favor this people.

This prayer then turns to Xenophon and his achievement. He has won both the stadion and the pentathlon at Olympia, a feat never before accomplished. In his own right he exemplifies Corinthian inventiveness with this "first-ever" achievement. But that is just the beginning. He has also won twice at the Isthmos and also at Nemea. His father's career was hardly less brilliant: an Olympic victory in the stadion, a double victory at Delphi in the stadion and diaulos, and in the same month a triple victory at the Athenian games. When Pindar turns to the other members of the immediate family, he finds their victories too numerous to count—like the sand of the sea. In the last triad of the poem he will return with a very impressive survey of the clan's victories.

The third and fourth triads are dedicated to Corinth's legendary heroes, who exemplify her qualities of mind (Sisyphos and Medea) and prowess (Glaukos). Glaukos figures prominently in the *Iliad*, and there (6.155–202) he tells of his grandfather Bellerophon. It is Bellerophon's story that Pindar chooses to narrate, and as usual he concentrates on one episode. Appropriately, it is his invention of the bridle, already mentioned as one of the Corinthian claims to fame. The narrative concentrates on the appearance of Athene to Bellerophon in a dream,[28] when she gives him the "charm for horses," thus permitting him to ride Pegasos and perform marvelous feats. In fact, although it is shorter, the catalog of his deeds is not unlike those of Xenophon and his family. But Pindar stops short of telling how Bellerophon died; we know from other sources (and from *Isth.* 7.45–47) that Bellerophon was carried away with his success and tried to ride Pegasos to heaven, but was thrown off. There is an implicit warning here for the Corinthians: the end of Bellerophon is an example of the *hybris* that their patron goddesses are said to ward off. As often, Pindar combines high praise with a reminder of man's limitations.

When Pindar returns to praise the clan (the Oligaithidai) in the fifth and final triad, he holds nothing back: besides the three Olympic victories of Xenophon and his father, they have won six Pythian crowns and sixty Isthmian and Nemean victories. The ensuing catalog of other places where they have won reads like a map of Greece, and it becomes—metaphorically—a flood out of which the poet must swim (he has already compared the number of their victories to the sand of the sea). All in all, the poem is a splendid illustration of Corinth's originality, as seen in her legendary hero Bellerophon and in her native son Xenophon and his family.

Nemean 10 to Theaios of Argos.   This is the only ode to a victor from Argos. Although it celebrates a victory in wrestling in local games in Argos and is not strictly a Nemean ode, we shall see that Theaios has plenty of Panhellenic victories to his credit. One unusual feature of this ode is the regularity with which the topics correspond to the triads. The first triad praises the city, the second the victor, the third his clan, and the fourth and fifth tell the story of Kastor and Polydeukes. Yet this regularity is offset by the unusual position of the narrative at the end of the ode. Only *Nem.* 1 also concludes with a major narrative.

The entire first triad consists of a catalog of Argive heroes that is reminiscent of, but even more impressive than, the catalog of Theban glories that opens *Isth.* 7.[29] Both odes have a similar movement from the praise of the city to the praise of the victor. In *Isth.* 7 the glories of Thebes are characterized from the start as "former" and in the transitional passage (16–19) their antiquity is stressed so that Pindar can emphatically introduce the recent victory of Strepsiades. In *Nem.* 10 the glories of Argos are characterized from the start as numerous and extensive ("thousands of achievements," 3; "long to tell," 4; "many cities," 5). This great quantity is then used in the transitional passage (19–20) to justify turning to the present victor:

> My mouth is too limited to recount all the glories
>   that belong to
> holy Argos; then, too, men's tedium is grievous
>   to encounter.

All these glories are beyond the capacity of the poet to relate or the audience to endure. Pindar suggests that his audience will appreciate his turning now to Theaios, another instance of Argive glory, whom he introduces with an emphatic "But nevertheless, wake the lyre" (21).

The victor is a true reflection of his city: he too has many achievements to relate. Besides victories at local and minor games, he has won one Pythian, three Isthmian, and three Nemean crowns. All he lacks is an Olympic victory, and Pindar prays to Zeus (the victor is tactfully portrayed as too shy to say it outright) that Theaios may go on to win this too.

The third triad catalogs the numerous victories of Theaios's clan, ending with "too many to count" (46). Pindar then observes that their remarkable athletic success is "no wonder" in view of the patronage of their clan by Kastor and Polydeukes, who join in their feasts.[30] Pindar notes that these gods "care greatly" (*perikadomenoi*) for just men and that gods are "faithful" (*piston*). These two qualities, "compassion" and "fidelity," are the keynotes of the following narrative of the friendship of Kastor and Polydeukes.

This story is one of the most impressive narratives in Pindar. The stately dactylo-epitritic meter, long periods, and alternating speeches give it a decidedly epic quality. As usual, Pindar sketches the main plot at the outset (55–59): the brothers spend alternate days in Hades and in Olympos, because when Kastor was killed in war, Polydeukes chose (*heileto*) this life rather than becoming completely divine himself. The key word is "chose," for the dramatic choice of Polydeukes is the high point of the narrative. After narrating the details of their fight with the giants Lynkeus and Idas that resulted in the mortal wounding of Kastor, the poet devotes the last triad entirely to the critical choice, where the two speeches dramatize the issues in Polydeukes' decision. No paraphrase could do justice to the nobility of Pindar's narrative (73–90):

Strophe 5

Polydeukes returned swiftly to his mighty brother
and found him not yet dead, but gasping hard for breath.
Hot indeed were the tears he shed; he groaned
and cried aloud, "Father Zeus, what release
will there ever be from sorrows? Let me also die
   with my brother here, O Lord.
Honor disappears when a man loses his friends and few
   mortals are faithful in time of toil

Antistrophe 5

and share the burden." Thus he spoke. And Zeus came before him
and said these words. "You are my son. But your brother

was conceived after you by your mother's husband,
when that hero came to her and sowed
his mortal seed. But nevertheless, listen; I grant you
this choice: if you prefer to escape death
    and hateful old age,
and come by yourself to live on Olympos with me and
    with Athene and dark-speared Ares,

Epode 5

this is yours to have. But if your struggle
is on your brother's behalf, and if you intend to share everything
    equally with him,
then you may live half the time beneath the earth
and half in the golden homes of Olympos."
When he heard these words, Polydeukes had no divided thoughts.
He released the eye, and then the voice,
    of bronze-armored Kastor.

"Greater love hath no man . . . ." Polydeukes asks, "What release will there ever be from sorrows?" (76–77), and at the end "He released the eye, and then the voice, of bronze-armored Kastor." The choice is no sooner offered than made.

Olympian 7 **to Diagoras of Rhodes.** Diagoras of Rhodes, a boxer, was one of the most prominent ancient athletes. Not only was he a great boxer in his own right, but his sons and grandsons were also Olympic champions. Cicero tells the following anecdote to illustrate the incredible success of the man (*Tusculan Disputations*, 1.111). When Diagoras witnessed his two sons win Olympic victories on the same day, a Spartan came up to him with these words of congratulations: "Die, Diagoras, for you will not reach heaven." In other words, Diagoras reached the limit of human success. All in all, three sons and two grandsons were Olympic victors. A famous story relates that Diagoras's daughter dressed as a trainer so that she could see her son win at the Olympic games. When she was discovered she faced a death penalty, but she was pardoned in view of the fact that she was the daughter, sister, and mother of Olympic victors.

The ode opens with an elaborate simile, in which Pindar compares his poetry to the wine in a golden goblet with which the father toasts his new son-in-law at his daughter's wedding. The majority of the ode is devoted to the legendary past of Rhodes. It is the only ode to a Rhodian and contains one of the most complex narratives in the odes.

There are actually three separate episodes: Tlapolemos's colonization of the island, the birth of Athene and the establishment of her cult there, and the birth of the island itself from beneath the sea. These narratives are remarkable for the fact that they are told in reverse chronological order and all three concern a disaster that turns into a success. At the end of the poem Pindar reviews Diagoras's spectacular career (80–87) and praises him for his noble qualities. The poem returns to joyful celebration at the end (the key word *charis* at 93 echoes lines 5 and 11), but, like the Spartan in Cicero's anecdote, Pindar concludes with a sobering reminder (94–95): "in a single space of time winds shift now here, now there."[31]

The scholia tell us that this poetic tribute to Rhodes and to one of her most distinguished citizens was engraved in golden letters and dedicated in the temple of Athene in Lindos (an important city on Rhodes).

Olympian 6 to Hagesias of Syracuse.   This ode celebrates a victory in the mule cart race, the least prestigious of the equestrian events.[32] The ode opens with an analogy from architecture, in which Pindar compares his introduction to a porch with golden columns on a splendid building. In other words, Hagesias's achievements are so spectacular that Pindar can begin right away with them: he is an Olympic victor, he is a custodial priest of the prophetic altar at Olympia, and is a "co-founder" of glorious Syracuse (4–9). Not only that, but he is a brave warrior—another Amphiaraos, who was both a prophet and a warrior. As B. L. Gildersleeve has pointed out,[33] the ode contains a remarkable number of pairs.

From his father's side Hagesias has inherited the prophetic gifts of the clan of the Iamidai. In one of his most celebrated narratives, Pindar tells of the birth of the clan's founder Iamos, whose mother was Euadne and father was Apollo. Of particular charm is the scene where the baby is hidden in bushes by his distraught mother, and "his tender body is bathed with yellow and deep purple light from violets" (55–56). When Iamos (named for "violets" *ia*) comes to maturity, he goes to Olympia and stands in the Alpheos River at night, praying to his grandfather Poseidon and father Apollo. Apollo's voice answers him and leads him to found his prophetic altar at Olympia, which was to be in the care of the Iamidai henceforth (57–71).

But from his mother's side, Hagesias has also inherited the martial and athletic prowess of Arkadia, for he has a second home in Arkadian Stymphalos. Pindar hopes that Hagesias will enjoy a warm reception when he arrives in Syracuse (lines 93–98 are a graceful tribute to Hieron) and compares his two homes to a ship's two anchors that keep it safe in a storm. This ode is a fitting tribute to a very versatile man.

Pythian 9 to Telesikrates of Kyrene. This is one of the most delightful of the odes. The main narrative concerns Apollo's intercourse with the nymph Kyrene, whom he would install as patron of the city of Kyrene along with the son she would bear him. The story is told in ring-composition.[34] It is full of sensitive character-drawing. The nymph grew up in the wilds of Thessaly, and was unlike other girls (18–22):

> She did not care for pacing back and forth at the loom,
> nor for pleasant meals with girl friends at home;
> no, with javelins and sword of bronze she would
> fight and kill the wild
> beasts.

In short, Kyrene has the same heroic spirit as Pelops in *Ol.* 1; she prefers the adventurous life of competition in the open to the security and pleasures of home. The "back and forth" of the loom strikingly depicts the routine, monotonous life of the stay-at-home.

When Apollo happens to see her wrestling bare-handed with a lion, he is astounded, and calls Cheiron out of his cave to ask if it is lawful for him to marry the girl. This conversation between Apollo and Cheiron (the prototypical matchmaker; see *Isth.* 8.38–45) is a masterpiece of sensitivity and wit.[35]

Indeed, marriage dominates the poem from beginning to end. Not only is there the "marriage" of Apollo and Kyrene, but during the catalog of Telesikrates' victories, Pindar pays him a graceful compliment by saying (97–100) that when the maidens saw him winning in the local games they prayed to have such a husband. And there is even the "extra" story at the end about how Telesikrates' ancestor won his bride in a footrace. As a consequence, some commentators have assumed that Telesikrates was about to be married. We have no way of knowing. This ode was probably composed around 474; it provides a glimpse of life in Kyrene very different from that in the two odes in the following decade to Arkesilas (*Pyth.* 4 and 5, discussed in chapter 5).

Nemean 11 to Aristagoras of Tenedos. Like the two preceding odes at the end of the Nemean collection, *Nem.* 11 does not celebrate a Nemean victory; in fact, it really does not celebrate a victory at all. It has been aptly called an "installation ode," for it is written on the occasion of Aristagoras's inauguration as president (*prytanis*) of the council on the island of Tenedos. Because Pindar relates that he was a very promising athlete as a youth and had won sixteen victories in local games, the ancient editors understandably placed it with the epinicians rather than, say, with the enkomia.

It opens with a hymn to Hestia, goddess of the hearth, asking her to admit Aristagoras to her council chamber.[36] The fact that the boy's parents held him back from competing in the major games forms the basis for Pindar's meditation on the relationship of hope, ambition, and success in the rest of the ode. The poet is convinced (and swears an oath to the effect) that Aristagoras could well have been victorious if he had gone to Delphi or Olympia. Pindar then muses that empty ambition makes one man fail, while lack of courage keeps another from winning what is properly his. The new councillor must mediate between these two extremes.

Pindar's praise of the young man bodes well for his success. He traces his lineage from Sparta and Thebes, he combines good looks and inborn determination, and he has potential for the highest athletic achievement. We gain the impression that Aristagoras knows the extremes of high ambitions stemming from natural talent as well as cautious limitation. If he can succeed in curbing ambition and striking a mean between too-hesitant hopes and empty-headed boasts, he may fulfill Pindar's prayer that he finish his year's term "with unscathed heart" (10). Aristagoras must seek "due measure" (*metron*, 47) when he faces the future in his deliberations on behalf of the city, as Pindar reminds him at the end of the ode (46–48).

> The streams of foreknowledge lie far off.
> One must seek due measure of gains.
> Too painful is the madness of unattainable desires.

***Olympians* 10 and 11 to Hagesidamos of Western Lokroi.** This complementary pair of odes celebrates a victory in the boys' boxing by Hagesidamos from Western (or Epizephyrian) Lokroi, an important athletic city of the early fifth century B.C. on the toe of Italy. Like other pairs of odes, these differ in length (*Ol.* 11 consists of a single triad; *Ol.* 10 has five) and in meter (*Ol.* 11 is in dactylo-epitritic, *Ol.* 10 is in Aeolic). The shorter ode, *Ol.* 11, has been thoroughly analyzed by E. L. Bundy,[37] so we shall concentrate on the longer one.

Ol. 10 is a remarkably complex poem that explores the relationship between memory and time.[38] Although many of Pindar's odes have dazzling introductions, this is one of the most surprising:

> Read me the Olympic victor's name,
> Archestratos's son, where it is written
> in my mind; for I owe him a sweet song
>   and have forgotten. O Muse, you and Truth,
> the daughter of Zeus, with a correcting hand
> absolve me from the charge of breaking a promise
> and harming a friend.
> For what was the future has come from afar
> and shamed my deep indebtedness.
>
> (1–8)

The "fiction" of this poem is that Pindar is late in composing the poem. In fact, so much time has gone by that he has actually forgotten about it and must have the details read to him from the record of his mind. The poem is a "debt" on which interest continues to accumulate over the passage of time, and the longer it continues, the deeper the debt and greater the shame. We cannot know the actual circumstances that occasioned this predicament (*Nem.* 3 also involves a late poem), but one can, I think, make a plausible guess. A look at the victory list for the 76th Olympiad in 476 reveals that Hagesidamos's victory in the boys' boxing occurred at the same time that Hieron won the horse race (celebrated in *Ol.* 1) and Theron won the chariot race (celebrated in *Ol.* 2 and 3). Naturally those patrons would take precedence over a boy boxer, and one could imagine a considerable delay before Pindar completed *Ol.* 10.

But more important is the use that Pindar makes of this situation in the poem itself. In the following lines he says that "interest" can clear him of reproach, and as a wave washes along a pebble, so he will pay off the debt with an "account of common concern as a loving kindness" (*philan . . . es charin*, 12). The language is full of double meanings from the vocabulary of business. The pebble that is washed along by the wave (of song) also connotes a "counter" used in calculations; the "account" (*logon*) has both senses of the English word: "story" and "business ledger." The "interest" that Pindar will pay on his debt will be the "account of common concern." Initially that applies to the forthcoming praise of the victor's city, but in a larger sense it includes the "account" of the first Olympic games later in the ode. And finally—

and most importantly—the last words take us beyond the realm of business: the poem will become a "loving kindness." We have noted before the importance of these two words in Pindar, *philos* and *charis*. They indicate that this poem will not be a grudging fulfillment of a mere contract, but will be done in the spirit of kindness and joy (*charis*) and out of friendship (*philos*).

After praising the city, the victor, and his trainer Ilas, Pindar announces his intention to tell of the founding of the Olympic games. Typically, the narrative proceeds quickly back in time to relate the events previous to the founding. Herakles had agreed to cleanse the great stables of Augeas, but after completing the work, the "friend-cheating" (*xenapatas*, 34) king refused Herakles' payment. Not only that, but Augeas's two nephews destroyed Herakles' army. Subsequently Herakles defeated them and their uncle as well. These negative examples provide a dark background as foil for the positive themes in the poem. In contrast to the "friend-cheating" Augeas, Pindar is concerned to absolve himself of "harming a friend" (*alitoxenon*, 6). Also, the "sheer death" (42) that Augeas could not escape contrasts with the "ruthless death " (105) from which Aphrodite rescues Ganymede at the end of the poem.

The middle strophe depicts the institution of the Olympic games. Herakles takes all the spoils won by defeating Augeas to Olympia, where he establishes the Olympic games. Several details are of importance. First, he pays proper respect to the gods by measuring out the sanctuary to his father Zeus. He also marks off a place for banquets and dedicates altars to the other gods, for this is a Panhellenic sanctuary. Then he names the nearby promentory "the Hill Kronos." Pindar informs us that it was previously "without a name" (*nōnymnos*, 51) during the reign of Oinomaos, when it was covered with deep snow. Then, at the first "birth-rites" of the games "the Fates were near at hand along with Time, who alone reveals incontrovertible truth" (51–55). And it was this Time that "revealed clearly in its onward course" (55) how Herakles established the festival. This statement rounds off the account of the founding of the games. Time and the Olympic festival are intimately connected. When we recall that the Greeks reckoned time by Olympiads and that recorded history began with the founding of the games, which recurred at regular intervals, then we see that Time was not only on hand at the "birth" of the games, but subsequently took on meaning itself. The deep snow that covered the "nameless" hill stands for the oblivion of undifferentiated nature with no regular ritual to distinguish time. Just as the hill gained a name through time at the institution of the games, so the victors also gained names that would last.

At this point Pindar surprisingly breaks in with a question (60): "Who won the new crown with his hands, or feet, or chariot?" Surely this is part of the "interest" on his debt, for he recounts the names of the (supposed) original victors in the various events (64–73). The program of the first games is then completed with the evening festival of enjoyment and song (73–77), and Pindar says that he will follow those first beginnings and now too "sing of Zeus as a namesake grace (*epōnymian charin*) of proud victory" (78–79). The "namesake grace" is the Olympic victory song. Once again, the words "name" and "grace" point to the dominant themes in the ode.

In the last triad Pindar recalls that this song has appeared "at last" (*chronōi*, "in time," 85). But by means of a simile (one of the few extended similes in the odes) he suggests that it was well worth waiting for (86–93).

> But as a son, born from his wife, is desired
> by a father already approaching the opposite of youth,
>   and the boy warms his mind with great love—
> since wealth that comes to be possessed
> by a stranger from outside
> is most hateful to a dying man—
> so, when a man performs noble deeds,
> Hagesidamos, and goes without song
> to the abode of Hades, vain are his aspirations
>   and brief is the joy he gains for his toil.

Indeed, the delay has made the song even more appreciated. The simile is extraordinarily precise: as the son inherits the father's wealth after his death, so the song preserves the legacy of noble deeds in posthumous fame. And Pindar assures the youth that this poem brings him "grace" (*charin*, 94) and tends his "fame" (*kleos*, 95). Then, after briefly praising the city for the last time, he turns to the victor with the final verses, full of love and warmth (99–105).

> I have praised the lovely son of Archestratos,
> whom I saw winning with his strong hand
> beside the altar at Olympia
> at that time;

> he was beautiful to see
> and had that youthful bloom that once
> rescued Ganymede from ruthless death
>   with the aid of Aphrodite.

Ganymede was a beautiful Trojan youth with whom Zeus fell in love. He took him to Olympos to be his immortal cupbearer. The reference is more than just a graceful compliment to the victor; it suggests that the poem (with the aid of the Muses) will also immortalize the young man as an act of love. What he did "at that time" (*chronon*, 102) is now preserved for time to come. Pindar has indeed "remembered" that "forgotten" Olympic victor, and through "grace" and "love" has rescued him from time's destruction. Pindar's "debt" has been paid with abundant "interest."

Chapter Seven

The Legacy of Pindar

Greek Literature

Although Pindar enjoyed great respect in antiquity, his influence is for the most part indirect. Since he and Bacchylides were the last genuine practitioners of elaborate choral lyric poetry, his art form essentially died with him and was never revived. Even the choral lyrics of Attic tragedy were greatly diminished in scope and importance by the end of the fifth century, while poets such as Philoxenos of Kythera and Timotheus of Miletos were composing a new form of monodic poetry.[1] Within forty years of Pindar's death the genre was moribund.

In the fourth century B.C., prose became the dominant medium. Plato shows admiration for Pindar's works and quotes him a number of times,[2] but the writer whose manner is closest to Pindar's is Isokrates. His eulogy of Euagoras (d. 374 B.C.), his treatises to Nikokles and Demonikos, and his address to Philip of Makedon (346 B.C.) are very reminiscent of Pindar's odes to Hieron. They, too, are "mirrors of princes." They show a similar blend of praise and counsel, while promoting heroic virtues and Panhellenic ideals.[3]

In the Hellenistic period (ca. 323–ca. 146 B.C.) two major poets show the influence of Pindar. Kallimachos (ca. 305–ca. 240 B.C.) adapted Pindaric elements in his hymns, and also wrote epinician poems to prominent Egyptians. Fragments of two of these poems, written in elegiac couplets, have survived on papyrus. One (fr. 384 Pfeiffer), of which about forty verses survive, celebrates the youthful victories of one Sosibios, while the other (just published in 1977) celebrates the Nemean chariot victory of Berenike (wife of Ptolemy III).[4] His contemporary, Theokritos, treats a number of Pindaric subjects. His panegyrics to Hieron II (*Idyll* 16; ca. 275 B.C.) and Ptolemy II (*Idyll* 17; ca. 273 B.C.) have many Pindaric qualities, but their form is entirely different. Gone is any trace of choral lyric; they are written in dactylic hexameter, the meter of epic, and are formally much closer to the Homeric Hymns.[5] His *Idyll* 24 is especially interesting, because it narrates Herakles' strangulation of the snakes, the same topic Pindar treats in *Nem.* 1. Here again the poem is in dactylic hexameter. The last forty lines are fragmentary, but the poem seems to end with a hope that the poet will win a reciting contest. It is apparent that while Pindar used the episode as part of a larger poem of praise, for Theokritos it becomes a detachable showpiece.[6]

Roman Literature

It was in Latin that Pindar found a most sympathetic reader, and (at times) almost a rival. As part of an Augustan revival of interest in pre-Hellenistic poets, Horace (65–8 B.C.) drew upon Greek classical models for the lyric poems in his four books of odes (which he called *carmina*, "songs"). He borrows the simpler verse forms of Greek monodic poetry (especially the four-line stanzas used by Sappho and Alkaios), and never attempts to write triadic choral lyric, which would have been extremely artificial in Latin. Many of his odes treat everyday subjects, but, as Quintilian says (10.1.96), *insurgit aliquando* "at times he rises to grandeur." When he does, Pindar is often his model.[7] We have already seen that he borrows the opening of his ode to Augustus (*Odes* 1.12) directly from the first two lines of *Ol.* 2: "quem virum aut heroa lyra vel acri . . . ."[8] Also in the grand Pindaric vein is the encomium on the military victory of a young nobleman, Drusus (*Odes* 4.4).[9] Of particular note in this poem is the very Pindaric reflection on the relationship of natural talent, training, and practice (4.4.33–34):

> doctrina sed vim promovet insitam,
> rectique cultus pectora roborant.
>
> But training improves natural strength
> and correct practices strengthen the heart.

We have already noted that the hymn to Calliope (*Odes* 3.4), one of the six so-called "Roman Odes" at the beginning of book 3, is modeled on *Pyth.* 1 and is in many ways his most ambitious Pindaric imitation.[10]

But Horace's greatest tribute to Pindar is *Odes* 4.2, which begins with his name: "Pindarum quisquis studet aemulari . . ." (Whoever strives to emulate Pindar, Iulus, relies on wings held together with wax through Daedalus's craft, and is bound to give his name to a transparent sea). The point is that any poet who attempts to rise through art to Pindaric heights will, like Icarus, plunge to failure. The next five stanzas—in one long sentence—sketch the style and content of Pindar's works. The first of those stanzas opens with the famous description of Pindar's style (verses 5–8).

> Like a river that rushes down from a mountain,
> which rains have swollen above its normal banks,
> so does Pindar rage and rush on with his
> deep voice.

Horace then characterizes the style of Pindar's dithyrambs with these words (10–12): "he tumbles new words through his daring dithyrambs and is carried along in rhythms freed from rules."

Horace's description of Pindaric style as a raging river without restraint has enjoyed a considerable influence and is greatly responsible for the view, prevalent from the Renaissance on, that Pindar's poems are lawless flights of enthusiasm with few—if any—restraints. Unfortunately, this passage is often taken from its context in the ode,[11] thereby creating a one-sided picture of Pindar. The ode itself is a familiar type known as a *recusatio*, a literary refusal to write in the grand style.[12] These *recusationes* are especially common in Augustan poetry and there are a number of them in Horace's odes.[13] In order to make a more effective contrast, they tend to exaggerate characteristics of the grand style, sometimes to the point of caricature. In this poem, Horace pictures Pindar as "the Swan of Dirce" flying among the clouds, while he himself is a small "bee from Mt. Matinus" that gathers honey along the banks of the Tibur River. Clearly this modest portrayal of himself (Rome's greatest lyric poet!) is as understated as his characterization of Pindar is exaggerated.[14]

But there is also a great deal of truth in the contrast between the two poets. From the point of view of a Horace working with precise and fixed metrical stanzas, the inventiveness of Pindaric meters and the freedom of Greek to invent new compound words must have appeared almost unlimited. This ode should be required reading for every student of English lyric poetry, for it contains the seminal discussion of the two principal types of odes bequeathed by the Graeco-Roman heritage. They came to be called the "greater" or Pindaric ode and the "lesser" or Horatian ode.

Also of great influence has been the description of Pindar in the famous sketch of Greek and Latin literature by Quintilian (ca. 30–100 A.D.): "Of the nine Greek lyric poets, Pindar is by far the greatest, for his magnificent spirit, his thoughts (*sententiis*), his figures of language, his tremendous abundance of matter and words, and his river (as it were) of eloquence; because of these traits, Horace rightly believed that no one could imitate him" (*Institutio Oratoria*, 10.1.61). In the treatise "On the Sublime" (by an anonymous author known as "Longinus," probably from the first century A.D.), Pindar is compared to a conflagration that burns up everything as it moves, and then inexplicably goes out and falls flat.[15] In this way, the ancient critical tradition established the notion that Pindar's verse was an undisciplined flood (or conflagration) of eloquence that often failed. Of great importance for reversing this judgment were Boeckh's rediscovery of Pindar's metrics in the early nineteenth century and Bundy's recovery of the generic conventions of the epinician ode in the mid-twentieth.

Renaissance to the Restoration

Through the publication of the Greek text of Pindar in the Aldine edition of 1513 and the Latin translation in the 1535 Basel edition, Pindar's work again became available to the literate community.[16] As might be expected, Italian poets were the first to be influenced by the reappearance of Pindar. Giangiorgio Trissino (1478–1550) and Luigi Alamanni (1495–1556) were the most important; the former combined the native canzone forms with triadic structure, while the latter adopted Pindaric form and style in his "Hymns," labeling the strophe, antistrophe, and epode "ballata," "contra-ballata," and "stanza."

But the first poet to make a serious effort to reproduce Pindaric odes in the vernacular was the most famous member of the French Pléiade, Pierre de Ronsard (1524–85). Although he ultimately renounced his ambition to be the "French Pindar," he published fourteen Pindaric odes in 1550. They vary in length and are written in short, rhymed lines (the short lines were undoubtedly inspired by the colometry of the early texts). They are remarkable pastiches of Pindaric topics.[17] In the preface to his books of odes, he says that he was particularly interested in conveying "les saintes conceptions de Pindare et ses admirables inconstances," the two traits of Pindar that future admirers and imitators would single out: his lofty sentiments and his sudden shifts.

Compared to France and Italy, England was late in discovering Pindar.[18] The early seventeenth-century editions of Erasmus Schmid (1616) and Iohannes Benedictus (1620) certainly made Pindar more readily available, and we know that John Milton owned and annotated a copy of Benedictus.[19] Although his "Nativity Ode" has a lofty Pindaric tone, there is little clear influence of Pindar on the content, and the form is an adaptation of Italian and Spenserian elements. In fact, considering Milton's close acquaintance with Pindar in the original Greek, it is surprising how little direct influence can be found throughout his works.

The first important Pindaric imitation in English is Ben Jonson's "To the Immortal Memory and Friendship of that Noble Pair, Sir Lucius Cary and Sir H. Morison," which was published in 1630. The poem is a consolation to Cary for the loss of his young friend Morison, who died at about twenty years of age. Its content is almost entirely borrowed from the Latin tradition, particularly from Seneca and later panegyric. Also evident is the tone of Roman satire in the portrayal of the worthless octogenarian (25–42) buoyed up by "the cork of title." But the form is very impressive, as one would expect from a master of English metrics like Jonson. The "Turns" and "Counter-Turns" (Jonson's terms for strophe and antistrophe) consist of rhymed couplets of iambic trimeter, tetrameter, and pentameter, while the "Stands" (i.e., epodes) include two dimeters and have a much more complex rhyme scheme. Altogether there are four triads with a very high degree of regularity. The intricate structure of rhythm and rhyme captures, as well as possible in English, the combination of creative freedom and demanding restraint that we saw in Pindar's odes. In addition, Jonson makes effective use of run-over from one stanza to the next (e.g., 32–33, 84–85, and 96–97), negative examples as "foil" (the infant and the octogenarian), and gnomes (e.g., "In small proportions we just beauty see, / And in short measures life may perfect be" [73–74]). All in all, the poem exhibits the ethical gravity and serious dignity of Pindar's odes, as well as complexity that rewards close rereadings.[20]

Jonson's experiment in strict Pindaric form was not duplicated for another century. Instead, Pindaric imitation took a new direction in 1656, when Abraham Cowley (1618–67) published his "Pindarique Odes, Written in Imitation of the Style and Manner of the Odes of Pindar."[21] The Preface begins with the famous statement: "If a man should undertake to translate Pindar word for word, it would be thought that one mad-man had translated another." Cowley begins his collection of odes with two close "imitations" of Pindar's *Ol.* 2 and *Nem.* 1. These are learned productions. In the accompanying notes (far longer than the translations themselves), Cowley provides the original Greek, a Latin translation (primarily based on Benedictus's edition), and extensive comments on his procedures. He states that his aim is not so much "to let the reader know precisely what he [Pindar] spoke, as what was his way and manner of speaking." Consequently, he takes many liberties with the text, including a total disregard for triadic form. Cowley was much influenced by Horace's description of Pindar in *Odes* 4.2., the first part of which he renders in the third ode in the collection as "The Praise of Pindar." As a result, he emphasized Pindar's "enthusiastical manner" and produced irregular and unpredictable stanzas very different from Pindar's controlled and disciplined form. In 1706 William Congreve criticized his neglect of triadic form,[22] and Samuel Johnson later blamed his irregular verse for providing too much license to inferior imitators.

Opinions vary considerably as to the success of his adaptations,[23] but in view of the popularity his odes enjoyed in his lifetime and their influence in English literature, it is worthwhile to look at one passage that imitates a Pindaric text we have already examined. The first stanza of "The Resurrection"—as Cowley himself points out—is an adaptation of the beginning of *Ol.* 11:[24]

> Not winds to voyagers at sea,
>   Nor showers to earth, more necessary be,
> (Heav'n's vital seed cast on the womb of earth
>   To give the fruitful year a birth)
>   Than verse to virtue; which can do
> The midwif's office, and the nurses's too;
> It feeds it strongly, and it cloaths it gay,
>   And when it dies, with comely pride
> Embalms it, and erects a pyramide
>   That never will decay
>   Till Heav'n it self shall melt away,
> And nought behind it stay.

In terms of form, Cowley keeps the structure of the priamel, but smoothes out Pindar's abruptness: not winds to voyagers . . . nor showers to earth . . . than verse to virtue. On the other hand, he follows Pindar's procedure of making each element longer than the preceding one. But most striking of all are Cowley's "metaphysical" elaborations. In Pindar's version the rains are simply called "children of the cloud." Cowley transforms this into an archetypal image of conception that is then followed by the metaphors of the midwife (6), the nurse (6), the embalmer (9), and the builder of the tomb (9). The stanza is organized by a carefully controlled series of metaphors and images from primal conception to the destruction of the world.[25] Within this framework comes the extravagant claim that verse (i.e., Cowley's) will survive until the end of time. This is witty poetry, full of playful conceits and clever adaptations of some Pindaric topics to mid-seventeenth-century tastes. As such, it deserves recognition for its achievements. But gone are the restraints of Pindaric form, the public occasion, the ethical seriousness, and the hard-won maturity of Pindar's thought.

The Restoration and Eighteenth Century

After Cowley, the Pindaric ode became a name for any poem of irregular form with pretensions to grandeur. Good examples in English are Dryden's "A Song for St. Cecilia's Day" (1687) and "Alexander's Feast" (1697).

Meanwhile, in France Pindar became a focal point of the dispute between Charles Perrault and Nicolas Boileau over the relative value of the "Ancients" and "Moderns." In his *Parallèle des Anciens et Modernes* (1692), Perrault had criticized Pindar for being so obscure that no one could understand him (3.160–63) and described his poetry as "galimatias impenetrable" (impenetrable nonsense [3.184]).[26] Boileau, the renowned translator of "Longinus," greatly appreciated the "sublime" effect in poetry, and as soon as volume 3 of Perrault's work appeared, he composed a poem "in the manner of Pindar" entitled "Ode sur la Prise de Namur" (1693), which he prefaced with a "Discours sur l'Ode." In it he continues the tradition of a Pindar carried away by poetic transport ("entièrement hors de soi"), who (paradoxically) breaks with reason in order to achieve more reason, and who produces a "beau désordre" (beautiful disorder) that is actually an effect of art. In his own ode, he aspires to be like Pindar ("rather pulled by the Demon of poetry than guided by reason") and attempts to achieve his "magnificent language" and "audacious figures." It is no surprise that his poem begins with the lines: "Quelle docte et sainte ivresse / Aujourd'hui me fait la loi?" (What learned and holy intoxication / Rules over me today?).

The most important Pindaric odes written in English in the mid-eighteenth century were "The Progress of Poesy" and "The Bard," published by Thomas Gray in 1757.[27] Each consists of three triads in regular (English) form that is reminiscent of Jonson's Cary-Morison Ode.

But the content has practically nothing to do with Pindar; in fact, the only notable connection is Gray's imitation of *Pyth*. 1 in the first antistrophe of "The Progress of Poesy."

> On Thracia's hills the Lord of War,
> Has curbed the fury of his car,
> And dropped his thirsty lance at thy command.
> Perching on the sceptered hand
> Of Jove, thy magic lulls the feathered king
> With ruffled plumes and flagging wing:
> Quenched in dark clouds of slumber lie
> The terror of his beak and lightnings of his eye.

"The Bard" (which stems from Gray's interests in Welsh poetry) is even more remote from Pindar; it consists of a dramatic tirade by a Welsh poet who commits suicide at the end of the poem. Gray was a learned scholar of antiquity,[28] but his odes demonstrate how Pindaric grandeur was being invoked for subjects totally alien to ancient Greece.[29]

The Romantics and Moderns

Coleridge's "Dejection: An Ode" and Wordsworth's "Intimations Ode" have often been called "Pindaric" odes.[30] By default, they are. In a tradition that inherited only two major models of the ode, the "greater" (Pindaric) and the "lesser" (Horatian), these poems are certainly more "Pindaric." Their lofty sentiments, grandeur, and formal irregularity certainly disqualify them from being "Horatian." But any resemblance to Pindar's poetry is very slight. The subjective romantic lyric is at the opposite end of the spectrum from Pindar's public celebratory poetry. Furthermore, Coleridge and Wordsworth did not really want to "Pindarize," a notion that had thoroughly exhausted itself in the poetry of Cowley, Collins, and Gray.

The early German romantics also greatly admired Pindar: Goethe, Schiller, and especially Hölderlin, who translated a number of Pindar's epinikia.[31] But the direct influence of Pindar on their poetry is very slight. As in the case of the English romantics, it was more the "grandeur" and Pindaric "spirit" that appealed to them.

A number of late romantic English poems, and even modern ones, are often considered "Pindaric." Among these are such diverse poems as Tennyson's "Ode on the Death of the Duke of Wellington" (1852), Gerard Manley Hopkins's "The Wreck of the Deutschland" (1875),

Matthew Arnold's "Westminister Abbey" (1881), and Allen Tate's "Ode to the Confederate Dead" (1928). These and others may be said to draw some distant inspiration from Pindar, but since the romantic period, the term "Pindaric" has become so vague as to be virtually useless. In some ways, the spirit of Pindar is more alive in the painstaking research of classical scholars than in the poetry of the last three centuries. Horace may well have had the last word; or as Cowley puts it in "The Praise of Pindar":

> Pindar is imitable by none:
> The Phoenix Pindar is a vast species alone.

Notes and References

Chapter One

1. There are five "lives" of Pindar: the Vita Ambrosiana, Vita Thomana, and Vita Metrica (A. B. Drachmann, ed., *Scholia Vetera in Pindari Carmina,* 3 vols. [Leipzig, 1903–27], 1:1–9), the entry in the *Suda* (a Byzantine lexicon), and the recently published portion of a life, POxy 2438, in *Oxyrhynchus Papyri*, vol. 26 (Oxford: Oxford University Press, 1961), 1–7. For a translation and discussion of the Vita Ambrosiana, along with a penetrating analysis of the contents of such lives, see M. R. Lefkowitz, *The Lives of the Greek Poets* (Baltimore, 1981), esp. 57–66, and 155–57. For a discussion of the content and methodology of the papyrus life, see E. G. Turner, *Greek Papyri* (Oxford: Oxford University Press, 1968), 105–6.

2. POxy 2438 (above, n. 1) refutes a view that Pindar died at age fifty and states that he won a dithyrambic contest in Athens in 496/5 (or possibly 497/6). This new evidence accords well with the traditional date of his earliest extant ode (*Pyth.* 10) as 498.

3. The Vita Ambrosiana quotes the following words to demonstrate that Pindar had special connections with Delphi: "the four-year festival celebrated with a procession of oxen, when I first slept as a beloved infant in swaddling-clothes" (fr. 193). We know that this "fact" was current in antiquity, for Plutarch mentions it in passing (see *Plutarch's Moralia*, vol. 9 [Cambridge, Mass.: Harvard University Press, 1961], 113–14), but scholars have become more and more skeptical about the first-person statements in Pindar as referring directly to the poet himself, and since we do not have the context from which the quote comes, it has a very dubious authority.

4. POxy 222: *Oxyrhynchus Papyri*, vol. 2 (Oxford: Oxford University Press, 1899), 85–95. This list is the most important piece of evidence for dating the odes.

5. We know that Aristotle compiled a list of Pythian victors, and presumably the dates recorded in the ancient commentaries (scholia) go back to this list, but there are enough discrepancies in the dating of Pythian odes to warrant extreme caution.

6. If we accept a statement in the first person at *Pyth.* 5.75 as referring to Pindar, then he was an aristocrat from the family of the Aigeidai, prominent in Sparta as well as in Thebes.

7. This version comes from the Vita Ambrosiana, which adds: "Others say that he dreamed his mouth was full of honey and wax and became a poet." Other versions are in the Vita Metrica, *Anth. Pal.* 16.305, and Pausanias 9.23.2. A similar story is even told of St. Ambrose.

8. See Hesiod, *Theogony* 22–34.

9. The story is related by Plutarch, *Moralia* 348A. See F. C. Babbitt, *Plutarch's Moralia*, vol. 4 (Cambridge, Mass.: Harvard University Press, 1957), 507.

10. For a sensitive analysis of these lines and of Pindar's use of the tradition, see B. Snell, "Pindar's Hymn to Zeus," in *Discovery of the Mind*, trans. T. G. Rosenmeyer (New York: Harper & Row, 1960), 71–89.

11. Two victory odes begin with this type of catalog: *Nem.* 10 and *Isth.* 7. See chapter 6.

12. Aristophanes, the Athenian comic playwright, alludes to this praise in his *Acharnians* (425 B.C.), and humorously suggests that the epithet "gleaming" might more appropriately describe sardines. The Athenian orator Isokrates says in his *Antidosis* (354 B.C.) that the Athenians gave Pindar ten thousand drachmas (probably a rhetorical exaggeration). The later accounts in the lives add the detail of the fine at Thebes.

13. Pausanias, *Description of Greece*, 10.24.5

14. The story is mentioned in numerous places: Plutarch, *Alexander* 11; Arrian, *History of Alexander* 1.9.10; Pliny, *Natural History* 7.29; and Dio Chrysostom 2.33. Some sources mention a previous sparing by Pausanias the Spartan.

15. W. J. Slater, "Pindar's House," *Greek, Roman, and Byzantine Studies* 12 (1971): 146–52.

16. *Isth.* 8.10; *Pyth.* 1.75–78; and *Isth.* 5.48–50.

17. Bronze Etruscan helmets from this engagement at Kyma, inscribed with dedications from Hieron and the Syracusians, have been found at Olympia.

18. Thukydides, *History of the Peloponnesian War* 2.41. The entire oration, with its grand portrayal of Athenian ideals and ambitions, provides an interesting contrast to the praise found in Pindar's odes.

19. Thukydides 1.70. The translation is that of R. Warner, *Thucydides: The Peloponnesian War* (New York: Penguin, 1972), 75–76.

Chapter Two

1. This list is taken from the Vita Ambrosiana; that given in the recently published papyrus life (POxy 2438) has a very different order and slightly different contents. For the Alexandrian classification of poetic genres, see H. Färber, *Die Lyrik in der Kunsttheorie der Antike* (Munich: Neuer Filser, 1936), who collects the ancient sources, and A. E. Harvey, "The Classification of Greek Lyric Poetry," *Classical Quarterly* 5 (1955): 157–75.

2. For a complete history of Pindar's text, see J. Irigoin, *Histoire du Texte de Pindar* (Paris, 1952). In the preface to his (lost) commentary on Pindar, Eustathios, the late twelfth-century Byzantine scholar, mentions that the epinikia were especially popular because they were more concerned with human affairs, contained fewer myths, and were not quite as obscure as the rest.

3. Originally published as POxy 841 by Grenfell and Hunt, *Oxyrhynchus Papyri* vol. 5 (Oxford: Oxford University Press, 1908). Although we have fragments for twenty-two paians, the most complete ones are 2, 4, and 6.

4. This is not to say that all the genres are totally uniform. From the scanty remains that we have, the *partheneia* appear to have a lighter tone with greater self-consciousness in the chorus of maidens, the *enkōmia* are more informal and contain many erotic touches (e.g., fr. 123) and the *thrēnoi* (e.g., fr. 129 and 133) contain eschatological elements.

5. Drachmann, *Scholia Vetera in Pindari Carmina*, 1:7.

6. These emendations are conveniently cataloged in D. E. Gerber, *Emendations in Pindar 1513–1972* (Amsterdam, 1976).

7. There has been considerable doubt whether *Isth.* 3 and 4 should be one poem or two, since both are in the same meter. For a discussion of the poems and arguments for their separation, see chapter 6.

8. The ancient scholia are collected and edited in Drachmann, *Scholia Vetera in Pindari Carmina.* The first volume contains the "lives," and the last volume has Eustathios's preface.

9. Ibid., 2:7 and scholium 1 a on p. 8.

10. E. L. Bundy, *Studia Pindarica,* 2 vols. (Berkeley, 1962).

11. For much more detailed information about Greek metrics in general, see T. G. Rosenmeyer, M. Ostwald, and J. W. Halporn, *The Meters of Greek and Latin Poetry* (Indianapolis: Bobbs Merrill, 1963). For a good brief account of Pindar's metrics with examples, see F. J. Nisetich, *Pindar's Victory Songs* (Baltimore, 1980), 31–39.

12. The evidence is collected and discussed by W. Mullen, *Choreia: Pindar and Dance* (Princeton, 1982), 225–30.

13. Ben Jonson used the terms "turn," "counter-turn," and "stand," in his Pindaric ode "To the Immortal Memory and Friendship of That Noble Pair, Sir Lucius Cary and Sir H. Morison." He undoubtedly borrowed them from the Italian. Nisetich, *Pindar's Victory Songs,* also uses them in his translation.

14. See G. Kirkwood, *Selections from Pindar* (Chico, Calif., 1982), 17: "[H]e 'comes' to celebrate the victory (*P.* 2.4) or 'sends' his poem (*P.* 2.68), and it is clearly impossible to rely on such phrases for evidence as to whether the poet himself was present on a given occasion." For an opposing view, see Mullen, *Choreia,* 25–31.

15. Translated by W. H. Fyfe, in *Aristotle, The Poetics; "Longinus" On The Sublime; Demetrius, On Style* (Cambridge, Mass.: Harvard University Press, 1932), 29.

16. Doric influence is most apparent in the use of a long *alpha* for the *eta* of Ionic Greek; for example, *areta* instead of *aretē* (excellence). As in the case of the other choral lyricists (Alkman, Stesichoros, Ibykos, Simonides, and Bacchylides) Pindar's language is a mixture of Ionic, Aeolic, epic, and Doric elements.

17. Horace's *Odes* exhibit a similar complexity of word order. If one

compares, for example, the opening strophe of 1.5, "Quis multa gracilis te puer in rosa" with Milton's famous adaptation, "Rend'red almost word for word," the greater flexibility of the inflected language will be apparent.

18. The comic playwright Aristophanes loves to parody Aischylos's magniloquent compound adjectives, but it is Pindar he parodies at *Birds* 943, where he speaks of "whirl-woven clothing." Unlike Pindar, Bacchylides frequently uses compound adjectives for chiefly decorative purposes, as in the description of the eagle's flight at 5.16–30.

19. The intricate word order of this phrase is noteworthy: "euphōnōn pterygessin aerthent' aglaais / Pieridōn." *Euphōnōn* goes with the last word *Pieridōn* "tuneful Pierian Maidens," *pterygessin* goes with *aglaais* "bright wings," and *aerthent'* "lifted up" is in the middle of this elaborate chiastic structure.

20. For many more examples, see W. H. Race, "Negative Expressions and Pindaric *Poikilia,*" *Transactions of the American Philological Association* 113 (1983): 99–100.

21. For more examples, see J. E. Sandys, *The Odes of Pindar* (Cambridge, Mass., 1937), xviii–xxi, and M. Simpson, "The Chariot and the Bow as Metaphors for Poetry in Pindar's Odes," *Transactions of the American Philological Association* 100 (1969): 437–73. For a general discussion, see R. Stoneman, "Ploughing a Garland: Metaphor and Metonymy in Pindar," *Maia* 33 (1981): 125–38.

22. See Race, "Negative Expressions," 95–122. All the positive aspects of "height," "brightness," and "sound" have their corresponding negative expressions.

23. Dionysios of Halikarnassos (ca. 10 B.C.) categorizes Pindar's style as "austere" and gives the following description of some verses from a dithyramb: "these lines are vigorous, weighty and dignified . . . though rugged, they are not unpleasantly so, and though harsh to the ear, are but so in due measure . . . they are slow in their time-movement, and present broad effects of harmony; and . . . they exhibit not the showy and decorative prettiness of our day, but the austere beauty of a distant past" (translated by W. R. Roberts, in *Dionysius of Halicarnassus On Literary Composition* [London: Macmillan, 1910], 217).

24. A great deal of Pindar's "imagery" comes from the natural environment, including plants, trees, leaves, and weather. See D. C. Young's analysis of *Ol.* 7 in his *Three Odes of Pindar* (Leiden, 1968), 69–105, and F. J. Nisetich, "The Leaves of Triumph and Mortality: Transformation of a Traditional Image in Pindar's *Olympian* 12," *Transactions of the American Philological Association* 107 (1977): 255–64.

25. F. Mezger, *Pindars Siegeslieder* (Leipzig: Teubner, 1880).

26. Most noteworthy are J. B. Bury, *The Nemean Odes of Pindar* (London, 1890) and *The Isthmian Odes of Pindar* (London, 1892), and M. R. Lefkowitz, *The Victory Ode* (Park Ridge, N. J., 1976) and "Pindar's *Nemean* XI," *Journal*

of Hellenic Studies 99 (1979): 49–56. The editions of C. A. M. Fennell, *Pindar: The Olympian and Pythian Odes* (Cambridge, 1893) and *Pindar: The Nemean and Isthmian Odes* (Cambridge, 1899) conveniently list the great majority of recurrent words and verbal echoes at the beginning of each ode.

27. The same qualities of language and style that we have observed in the victory odes are evident throughout the remains of the other poems that we have. Pindar's style is remarkably consistent, and it is clear why the Alexandrian editors based their classifications on content rather than on style.

Chapter Three

1. Light is probably the dominant image/symbol in Pindar, as perhaps in Greek literature generally. Greek is especially rich in words denoting "light," and they constitute one of Pindar's major sources for metaphors. See H. Gundert, *Pindar und sein Dichterberuf* (Frankfort: Klostermann, 1935), 1–29.

2. See *Ol.* 5.5, 6.69; *Pyth.* 10.24; and *Nem.* 10.32. A number of good books have been written on Greek athletics and the Olympic games, among which I would single out M. I. Finley and H. W. Pleket, *The Olympic Games: The First Thousand Years* (New York, 1976) and N. Yalouris, *The Olympic Games* (Athens: Ekdotike Hellados, 1976), the latter especially for its reproductions of vase paintings. The ancient section of this work is also available as *The Eternal Olympics* (New Rochelle, N. Y., 1979).

3. See Finley and Pleket, *The Olympic Games,* 63: "Those who survived the preliminary investigations [for eligibility] spent a full month in training under strict supervision, having sworn by Zeus Horkios that they had already been training during the whole of the previous ten months."

4. For more information concerning the events at Olympia, see Finley and Pleket, "The Olympic Programme," in *The Olympic Games,* 26–46. Of the pentathlon, they say (34): "Victory was not calculated on points. If anyone was first in three events, that automatically ended the contest. Otherwise the field was reduced for the final contest, the wrestling (in which three falls were required for victory), to those competitors who still had a chance to win because of their placing in the four completed events."

5. The total number of odes to victors in the gymnastics events is actually 25, for *Ol.* 13 celebrates a double victory in the pentathlon and stadion. *Pyth.* 12, a victory in flute playing, and *Nem.* 11, an installation ode, bring the total number of odes to 45.

6. In the "crown" games there were only first-place winners. Although the other major games eventually had separate competitions for "youths" (*ageneioi,* "beardless") in their late teens, Olympia maintained only the boys' division (in the stadion, wrestling, and boxing).

7. See D. C. Young, "Panathenaic Prizes in the Classical Period," in *The Olympic Myth of Greek Amateur Athletics* (Chicago: Ares, 1984), 115–27,

who estimates that the top prizes in today's dollars would be worth some $40,680 for the pentathlon, wrestling, and boxing, $67,800 for the stadion, and $94,920 for the four horse chariot race.

8. A fragment of a marble stele from about 334 B.C. was found at Delphi, which thanks Aristotle and his student Kallisthenes for having compiled a list of victors in the Pythian games. See M. N. Tod, *A Selection of Greek Historical Inscriptions* (Oxford: Oxford University Press, 1948), 2:246–48.

9. See *Sextus Julius Africanus: List of Olympian Victors*, ed. I. R. Rutgers (1862; reprint, Chicago: Ares, 1984).

10. POxy 222, *Oxyrhynchus Papyri*, 2:85–95.

11. There is an epitaph attributed to Simonides (*Anth. Pal.* 13.14) for Dandis of Argos that records two Olympian victories, three Pythian, two Isthmian, fifteen Nemean, and innumerable others. For the remarkable career of Astylos of Syracuse (and Kroton), see Young, *The Olympic Myth*, 141–44.

12. There is some doubt about the restoration of the name Theognetos in the papyrus.

13. An inscription from Delphi of the early fourth century B.C. records victories at Olympia in both boxing and the pankration, three Pythian victories (one uncontested), ten Isthmian victories (one in the pankration), nine Nemean, and a total of 1,300 victories in a twenty-two year career. For details, see J. Ebert, *Griechische Epigramme auf Sieger an gymnischen und hippischen Agonen* (Berlin: Akademie Verlag, 1972), 118–26. The second-century A.D. writer Pausanias (6.11.2–9) tells how the Thasians came to worship Theagenes and puts the total number of his victories at 1,400. Young, *The Olympic Myth*, 144 argues for the validity of these enormous figures.

14. Pindar also uses the words *kōmos* (victory procession, revel) and *melos* (song). The first emphasizes the festive carousal, the second the melodious singing.

15. Some versions add a moralizing conclusion to the story. During the ensuing celebration, two young men came to the door of the palace and asked to speak with Simonides. When he went out they disappeared, and the roof collapsed on the guests.

16. See H. Fränkel, "The 'Powers' in Pindar," in *Early Greek Poetry and Philosophy*, trans. M. Hadas and J. Willis (Oxford, 1975), 481–488.

17. For bibliography and a discussion of some features of Greek hymns, see W. H. Race, "Aspects of Rhetoric and Form in Greek Hymns," *Greek, Roman, and Byzantine Studies* 23 (1982): 5–14.

18. For the connection of Hestia with council-chambers, see R. E. Wycherley, *How the Greeks Built Cities* (New York: Norton, 1976), 132–42 and S. G. Miller, *The Prytaneion: Its Function and Architectural Form* (Berkeley: University of California Press, 1978), 13–16.

19. In the analysis of *Pyth.* 1 in chapter 4 we shall see how prayers articulate an ode by introducing and concluding topics.

20. The ground-breaking work on Pindaric ring-composition was in the

dissertation of L. Illig, *Zur Form der pindarischen Erzählung* (Berlin: Junker & Dünnhaupt, 1932). R. Hamilton, *Epinikion: General Form in the Odes of Pindar* (The Hague, 1974), 56–78, provides helpful schematic comparisons of narrative structures in various odes.

21. The Greek term *kephalaion* (heading) is often used to describe this summary of the story. See Hamilton, *Epinikion*, 61–65.

22. Verbal echoes occur throughout odes, but sometimes they clearly are intended to underscore a completed "ring." Unfortunately, these subtle effects of language are usually lost in translations.

23. This dramatic episode was a favorite theme of Greek art. For an example from a vase painting, see Nisetich, *Pindar's Victory Odes*, 229.

24. The poetic model is, of course, the catalog of ships in *Iliad* 2.

25. For a survey of the priamel, see W. H. Race, *The Classical Priamel from Homer to Boethius* (Leiden: Brill, 1982).

26. See W. H. Race, "Pindar's 'Best is Water': Best of What?" *Greek, Roman, and Byzantine Studies* 22 (1981): 119–24.

27. One small episode in the "Quarrel between the ancients and moderns" concerns the comprehensibility of the opening of *Ol.* 1. See Boileau's "Réflexion VIII," which appeared in 1694 and defends the integrity of the text against Charles Perrault's charges that Pindar's verse was "nonsense."

28. E. L. Bundy's *Studia Pindarica* and "The 'Quarrel Between Kallimachos and Apollonios,' Part I: The Epilogue of Kallimachos's *Hymn to Apollo*," *California Studies in Classical Antiquity* 5 (1972): 39–94, show in great detail how Pindar modifies and varies standard topics.

Chapter Four

1. For the historical background of this ode, see chapter 1. There have been many translations of this famous poem (especially of its opening hymn), and numerous articles deal with its artistry. For the general reader, I might mention R. A. Brower, "The Theban Eagle in English Plumage," *Classical Philology* 9 (1940): 25–30 and R. V. Schoder, "The Artistry of of the First Pythian Ode," *Classical Journal* 38 (1943): 401–12.

2. For a good explanation of the meter in *Pyth.* 1, see Nisetich, *Pindar's Victory Songs*, 37–39.

3. Greek literature frequently describes a subject indirectly by portraying its effects on others. A classic example is the effect of Helen's beauty on the old men on the wall of Troy at *Iliad* 3.154–60. Others include Sappho's reaction to seeing her beloved in fr. 31 and Pindar's to the beauty of Theoxenos in fr. 123.

4. If the Lyre can pacify the "heart" of the most violent of the gods, Ares, then *a fortiori* it can soothe the "minds" of the other gods.

5. Music also has a martial aspect and was used to lead troops into

battle. Some of the martial poetry of Tyrtaios and Kallinos is still extant. The Greeks often sang a paian when going into battle, and Pindar's second *Paian* was composed for the citizens of Abdera in the hopes that they would win a decisive battle over the neighboring Thracians. In a martial context, the word "terrified" connotes panic and flight.

6. For another account of Typhon, see Hesiod, *Theogony* 820–80.

7. Seneca calls the description of Mt. Aitna's eruption "every poet's commonplace" (*Epis.* 79.5). Some versions include Aischylos, *Prometheus Bound* 353; Lucretius, *De Rerum Natura* 6.639; and Vergil, *Aeneid* 3.570. A six-hundred line poem *Aetna* in Latin is extant, and as late as 400 A.D. Macrobius was comparing Vergil's version with Pindar's (*Saturnalia* 5.17.8–14).

8. See 18. In addition, three words in this line begin with "ph" (which in Greek was no doubt more plosive than our "ph").

9. The poet has withheld the last item "with the chariot" (the chariot race was the most prestigious of the equestrian events) for a climactic enjambment at the beginning of the epode.

10. Hieron founded Aitna with 5,000 settlers drawn from Sicily and 5,000 from the Peloponnesos. What better way to advertise his new city than to have it heralded at the Panhellenic games, especially at Delphi, which had played such an important role in colonization during the previous centuries? Pindar's phrasing subtly suggests the surprise the herald's words would have had on the gathering; he was well known as Hieron of Syracuse—this victory was for Aitna. The later Greek historian Diodorus Siculus tells us that Hieron died in Aitna (in 467 or 466) and received heroic honors as the founder of the city (11.66.4).

11. Note the use of the gnome and the prayer to complete the section on the city and form a transition to praise of Hieron, which is in turn introduced by a gnome ("For the gods provide all the means for human achievements") and the poet's "prayer" ("I hope") that he will perform adequately.

12. See M. R. Lefkowitz, "The Poet as Athlete," *Journal of Sport History* 11 (1984): 18–24.

13. For a brief discussion of the possibilities, see R. W. B. Burton, *Pindar's Pythian Odes* (Oxford, 1962), 102–3, who argues that Hieron's campaign against Akragas is the most likely one meant here.

14. Examples include: *Ol.* 2.83–100, 6.1–4, 9.35–41, 9.100–108, 13.93–97; *Pyth.* 4.247–248, 8.29–34, 9.76–79, 10.51–54, 11.38–42; *Nem.* 4.33–43, 5.16–21, 6.53–57, 10.19–22. Pindar writes more self-consciously than any other Greek lyric poet we know. He constantly engages the reader in the act of composition.

15. As a poet of praise, Pindar was particularly concerned with the "envy" (*phthonos*) that so often is aroused by someone's success. It was especially prevalent in the Greek competitive culture, and it is constantly mentioned by speakers and poets. An excellent example is the opening of Perikles' "Funeral Oration" (in Thukydides, *History of the Peloponnesian War*, 2.35),

where he fears that some in his audience might, through envy, disbelieve his high praise.

16. This gnome is also quoted at Herodotos 3.52.

17. The translation is that of J. H. Freese, in *Aristotle, "Art" of Rhetoric* (Cambridge, Mass.: Harvard University Press, 1939), 101–2.

18. Herodotos tells the story of Kroisos in the first book of his *Histories*. Bacchylides tells a different version of Kroisos's death in his third epinician ode, composed for Hieron when he won the Olympic chariot race in 468. In it he implies that Hieron is a Greek Kroisos, for when he finishes the story of Kroisos he says, "Of all the men in Hellas, glorious Hieron, none will dare claim that he has sent more gold than you to Delphi." Through his splendid gifts and dedications to Delphi, Hieron was clearly patterning himself after Kroisos. But while Bacchylides trumpets the fact, Pindar characteristically plays it down by his depiction of the negative example of Phalaris.

19. Phalaris is said to have first tried it out on the architect who built it for him. The great bull has overtones of Carthaginian "baalism," and suggests that Phalaris, like the enemies of Zeus, is beyond the pale of Greek civilization.

20. We have mentioned the martial aspects of music and poetry (see above, n. 5). The lyre's possessor, Apollo, wields both the bow and the lyre. Music and poetry played a much more public and active role in ancient Greece than they do today.

21. The lyric poem in Latin that comes closest is Horace's "Descende caelo et dic age tibia . . ." (*Odes* 3.4). For an excellent analysis of the poem and its close relationship with *Pyth.* 1, see E. Fraenkel, *Horace* (Oxford: Oxford University Press, 1957), 273–85.

22. D. C. Young, "Pindar *Pythians* 2 and 3: Inscriptional *pote* and the 'Poetic Epistle,'" *Harvard Studies in Classical Philology* 87 (1983): 31–42 refutes the use of *pote* to justify a late dating of the ode and questions the validity of calling it a "poetic epistle." His *Three Odes of Pindar*, 27–68, provides a fundamental analysis of *Pyth.* 3 and the present discussion is greatly indebted to it.

23. Hesiod's version of the story relates that Apollo was informed by the raven, which was formerly white, but because of its evil tidings, the god changed its color to black. Young, *Three Odes of Pindar*, 37–38, discusses how and why Pindar adapted the earlier version.

24. See ibid., 27–68 and app. 1 for a catalog of the theme of the near and the far in numerous Greek authors.

25. See ibid.

26. The gnome recommends the Greek virtue of *sōphrosynē*, wise restraint. In line 63, Cheiron is called "wise" *(sōphrōn)*. For an excellent survey of the concept of *sōphrosynē*, see H. North, *Sophrosyne: Self-Knowledge and Self-Restraint in Greek Literature* (Ithaca, N.Y.: Cornell University Press, 1966).

27. See 63.

28. Slater, "Pindar's House," reviews the evidence and suggests that the reference might be to Demeter in Syracuse.

29. Young, *Three Odes of Pindar*, 48–49.

30. For a brief sketch of this topic, see E. R. Curtius, *European Literature and the Latin Middle Ages*, trans. W. R. Trask (New York: Harper & Row, 1963), 80–82.

31. These weddings are meant to contrast with the "wedding" Koronis could not wait for.

32. It is interesting that the ode contains three pairs of examples: Koronis-Asklepios, Peleus-Kadmos, and Nestor-Sarpedon.

33. Medicine is one of Pindar's favorite metaphors for the power of poetry to alleviate the pain of hard work and to provide a kind of remedy for mortality. A good example is the opening of *Nem.* 4.

34. See 9.

35. For the analysis of this priamel, see 34–35.

36. The phrase comes from R. C. Jebb, "Pindar," *Journal of Hellenic Studies* 3 (1882): 168.

37. Among a great deal of work, I would single out D. E. Gerber, *Pindar's Olympian One: A Commentary* (Toronto, 1982), and A. Köhnken's articles, "Pindar as Innovator. Poseidon Hippios and the Relevance of the Pelops Story in Olympian 1," *Classical Quarterly* 24 (1974): 199–206 and "Time and Event in Pindar O. 1.25–53," *Classical Antiquity* 2 (1983): 66–76. Young, *Three Odes of Pindar*, app. 2, outlines the extremely complex structure of *Ol.* 1.

38. For an analysis of this transitional passage, see A. M. Miller, "Pindar, Archilochus and Hieron in P. 2.52–56," *Transactions of the American Philological Association* 111 (1981): 135–43.

39. See E. Thummer, "Die zweite pythische Ode Pindars," *Rheinisches Museum* 115 (1972): 293–307.

40. We cannot know how much Pindar idealized his patron, and a man as powerful as Hieron was bound to have bitter enemies. The historian Diodorus Siculus, writing in the first century B.C., gives a very different assessment (11.67.3–4): "Gelon was beloved by all for his gentleness and he lived in peace the rest of his life. But Hieron, the oldest of his brothers, ruled differently: he was greedy and brutal; in short, he was totally devoid of sincerity and noble qualities" (*kalokagathia*).

41. The term comes from W. Jaeger's excellent presentation of Pindar's educational intention in his *Paideia: The Ideals of Greek Culture*, trans. G. Highet (Oxford, 1945), 1:205–22. These "mirrors of princes" will have a long history in prose from Xenophon (whose *Hieron* is a fictitious dialogue between Hieron and Simonides) and Isokrates (who, like Pindar, also addressed kings) into the Renaissance, with Erasmus's *Institutio Principis Christiani*. See L. K. Born, *The Education of a Christian Prince by Desiderius Erasmus* (New York: Norton, 1968), 44–130, and M. P. Rewa, *Reborn as Meaning: Panegyrical Bi-*

ography from Isocrates to Walton (Washington, D.C.: University Press of America, 1983).

Chapter Five

1. Not long afterward (probably in 474) in a dithyramb (fr. 76) Pindar praised Athens as "the bulwark of Hellas" for her role in defeating the Persians.

2. One word sums up this tragic view of life: "ephemeros" (subject to the vicissitudes of the day). See H. Fränkel, "Man's 'Ephemeros' Nature According to Pindar and Others," *Transactions of the American Philological Association* 77 (1946): 131–45. The space of a day is the critical time for humans. We have "daily" needs, and a day can completely reverse our fortunes. We cannot clearly foresee tomorrow, and therefore we must "live for the day" (*carpe diem* in Horace's pithy expression at *Odes* 1.11.8) and make use of present good fortune. In the gnome at *Ol.* 2.32–33 Pindar says that we cannot know if we will ever complete a day with unimpaired happiness.

3. See L. Woodbury, "Equinox at Acragas: Pindar, *OL.* 2.61–62," *Transactions of the American Philological Association* 97 (1966): 597–616, and F. Solmsen, "Two Pindaric Passages on the Hereafter," *Hermes* 96 (1968): 503–6.

4. The meaning of "with equal nights and with equal days" is much debated, but L. Woodbury, "Equinox," argues very persuasively that it depicts an eternal equinox in this first stage of blessedness.

5. Many similar elements are found in the "myths" at the end of Plato's *Gorgias* and *Republic*. Also very interesting is the direct quotation from one of Pindar's dirges (fr. 133) by Plato at *Meno* 81B. Pindar was clearly one of Plato's favorite poets and one he consistently treats with respect.

6. This is a very difficult passage. See W. H. Race, "The End of *Olympia* 2: Pindar and the *Vulgus*," *California Studies in Classical Antiquity* 12 (1979): 251–67.

7. Others include *Ol.* 9.100–104, *Nem.* 3.40–42, 4.33–43. For the last, see A. M. Miller, "*N.* 4.33–43 and the Defense of Digressive Leisure," *Classical Journal* 78 (1983): 202–20.

8. Pindar artfully holds off the name until the last word of the long sentence (90–95) and gives it even greater emphasis by enjambing it as the first word of the epode. On the whole, Pindar is sparing in these grand gestures, usually preferring subtler nuances.

9. Here *areta* manifests itself as generosity to friends, as in the case of Theron (in *Ol.* 2) and the *philophrōn areta* (loving-minded excellence) of Kroisos (*Pyth.* 1.94).

10. Modern readers, used to sensationalism in sports reporting, are surprised to find so few details about the events themselves. Although there is an exciting narration of a Pythian chariot race in Sophokles' *Elektra* 680–763,

it was the Hellenistic and Roman periods that most delighted in the thrilling details. The calm repose of the *Charioteer of Delphi* (see frontispiece) after the race fittingly represents the important moment for Pindar.

11. The mention of Apollo's oracle (*mantēion*) in 69 completes a ring with the oracles (*manteumasin*) in 62 and marks off this section concerned with Apollo's aretalogy.

12. There has been considerable controversy about the reference of the "I" in this passage, and elsewhere, whether it refers to the person of the poet or to the chorus. Most take it to apply personally to Pindar here. See M. R. Lefkowitz, "*Tō Kai Egō*: The First Person in Pindar," *Harvard Studies in Classical Philology* 67 (1963): 230–32. For an opposing view, see Fränkel, *Early Greek Poetry*, 427, n. 2.

13. Compare the word *philos* (my friend) at *Iliad* 9.601 at the end of Phoinix's speech of advice to Achilles and *ō phile* to Hieron at *Pyth.* 1.92.

14. Two books among many on this subject are Lord Ragland, *The Hero: A Study in Tradition, Myth, and Drama* (London: Methuen, 1936), and J. Campbell, *The Hero of a Thousand Faces* (New York: Bollingen, 1949). For brief introductions, see Lord Ragland, "The Hero of Tradition," *Folklore* (1934): 212–31, and A. Taylor, "The Biographical Pattern in Traditional Narrative," *Journal of the Folklore Institute* 1 (1964): 114–29.

15. For the motif of others' reactions, see chap. 4, n. 3.

16. B. L. Gildersleeve, *Pindar: The Olympian and Pythian Odes* (New York, 1885), 278.

17. E. Robbins, "Jason and Cheiron: The Myth of Pindar's Fourth Pythian," *Phoenix* 29 (1975): 205–13, discusses the presence of medical terms in the ode and draws attention to the significance of the names of Jason ("Healer") and Cheiron ("Handy"). Cheiron was famous for teaching medicine (to Asklepios and Achilles) and in line 271 Pindar refers to a "gentle hand to tend a sore wound."

18. See C. Carey, "The Epilogue of Pindar's Fourth Pythian," *Maia* 32 (1980): 143–52.

19. See chap. 4, n. 41.

20. The complexity of one sentence (16–17) is analyzed on 15.

21. The same theme underlies the statement in *Ol.* 2.56, "If a man has it (wealth) and knows the future . . . ."

22. See chapter 3.

23. See 76 and chap. 4, n. 3. Bundy, *Studia Pindarica*, 3, notes the frequent use in Pindar of "wonder" to mark the climax of a scene. As the "wonder" of the onlookers ended the tableau of erupting Mt. Aitna in *Pyth.* 1.26–28, so here the "wonder" of Amphitryon concludes the scene with the snakes.

24. This analogy is implicit in *Pyth.* 1. For a brief discussion of the association of the Parthenon metopes with triumph over the Persians, see J.

J. Pollitt, *Art and Experience in Classical Greece* (Cambridge: Cambridge University Press, 1972), 80–82.

25. The remains of Pindar's *enkōmia* and *skolia* are collected and analyzed in B. A. van Groningen, *Pindare au Banquet* (Leiden: A. W. Sythoff, 1960).

26. There is a lost work called "The Precepts of Cheiron," and this precept was perhaps drawn from it. Throughout the *Iliad* Achilles shows a strong sense of filial devotion to both of his parents.

27. For a more detailed analysis of this passage, see chapter 3.

28. For other instances of the four cardinal virtues in Pindar, see H. North, "Pindar, *Isthmian*, 8, 24–28," *American Journal of Philology* 69 (1948): 304–8.

29. Many cups bear dedicatory inscriptions to a *kalos* (beautful boy). This homosexual love finds its prose expression in such dialogues as Plato's *Charmides, Lysis,* and *Symposium* and in the "Erotic Essay" attributed to Demosthenes.

30. For analyses of this opening section and its relationship to the rest of the poem, see L. Woodbury, "Pindar and the Mercenary Muse. *Isthm.* 2.1–13," *Transactions of the American Philological Association* 99 (1968): 527–42, and F. J. Nisetich, "Convention and Occasion in *Isthmian* 2," *California Studies in Classical Antiquity* 10 (1977): 133–56.

31. The view of one scholiast (Kallistratos) that Pindar was covertly requesting back payment that Xenokrates had owed him has been accepted by some modern commentators. Such ridiculous "gossip" has been one of the greatest stumbling blocks for the correct interpretation of Pindar—in antiquity and still today. For another example, see 10.

32. Like *Pyth.* 3 it was classed among odes celebrating chariot victories purely on artificial grounds.

33. See also *Nem.* 9.53–55 and, for an analogy from long jumping, *Nem.* 5.19–20.

34. See Nisetich, "Convention and Occasion," 147, 155, n. 64.

Chapter Six

1. Although there is some doubt, *Pyth.* 8 is probably to a boy victor.

2. Melesias is also praised in two other odes to Aiginetans, *Nem.* 4.93 and 6.68. Menander, another trainer from Athens, is praised in *Nem.* 5.48 and in Bacchylides 13.192 (both for an Aiginetan victor). Two other trainers are mentioned in the odes: Orseas (*Isth.* 4.72) and Ilas (*Ol.* 10.17).

3. For the combination of talent, instruction, and practice in Greek educational theory, see P. Shorey, "*Physis, Meletē, Epistēmē,*" *Transactions of the American Philological Association* 40 (1909): 185–201.

4. At *Isth.* 5.54–58 Pindar praises them for their long effort and ex-

penses, and says that they serve as an example for others who aspire to athletic prominence.

5. Hesiod, *Works and Days* 412; literally, "practice (*meletē*) aids performance."

6. At *Ol.* 10.20–21 Pindar again uses the metaphor of the whetstone for training: "If one has inborn excellence (*aretāi*), another man may whet him and urge him on to prodigious fame—with god's help." Here are all the components of victory: natural gifts, training, encouragement, and god's helping hand (we usually call it good luck).

7. Ships and chariots are traditionally an awe-inspiring sight. They also appear in the priamel in Sappho, fr. 16: "Some say a host of horsemen, others of infantry, and others of ships is the most beautiful thing on the black earth; but I say it is what one loves." At the end of the fragment, Sappho refers specifically to Lydian chariots.

8. See 34–35. Gold and the sun also appear in both passages.

9. For an excellent discussion of this passage, see Fränkel, *Early Greek Poetry*, 485–88. He points out the similarity to Sappho, fr. 16.

10. Herodotos also tells that before the Battle of Salamis, the Greeks called upon Ajax and Telamon to come to their aid and sent a ship to Aigina to bring the images of Aiakos and his sons (8.64).

11. For a brief account of the controversy and a lengthy discussion of Neoptolemos in the poem, see. L. Woodbury, "Neoptolemus at Delphi: Pindar, *Nem.* 7.30 ff.," *Phoenix* 33 (1979): 95–133. Also see the analysis of Kirkwood in *Selections from Pindar*, 257–76.

12. See 28–29.

13. For darkness and light as frequent metaphors in Pindar, see chapter 2. For an illuminating discussion of action in the public realm and its need for permanence in works of art, see Hannah Arendt, *The Human Condition* (Chicago: University of Chicago Press, 1958), especially 1–96.

14. These are some suggestions for further reading about odes only touched upon here: *Pyth.* 8: Burton, *Pindar's Pythian Odes*, 174–93; *Nem.* 3: H. Erbse, "Pindars dritte nemeische Ode," *Hermes* 97 (1969): 272–91; *Nem.* 4: A. M. Miller, "N. 4.33–43 and the Defense of Digressive Leisure," *Classical Journal* 78 (1983): 202–20; *Nem.* 8: A. M. Miller, "*Phthonos* and *Parphasis*: The Argument of *Nemean* 8.19–34," *Greek, Roman, and Byzantine Studies* 23 (1982): 111–20; *Isth.* 8: A. Köhnken, "Gods and Descendants of Aiakos in Pindar's Eighth Isthmian Ode," *Bulletin of the Institute of Classical Studies* 22 (1975): 25–36 and D. C. Young, "Pindar," in *Ancient Writers*, ed. J. T. Luce (New York, 1982), 1:164–65.

15. See Fränkel, "Man's 'Ephemeros' Nature."

16. For the Olympic victor list of 476 and the epigram for Theognetos, see 22–23.

17. See 22.

18. Although it is far from certain, most scholars now accept the date

given in the scholia for this ode as 446. If this is correct, then it is the last datable ode that we have.

19. Young's brilliant essay on this poem in *Three Odes of Pindar*, 1–26 reversed the evaluation of this ode. The following analysis relies heavily on his interpretation.

20. See W. H. Race, "Some Digressions and Returns in Greek Authors," *Classical Journal* 76 (1980): 1–8.

21. Pindar addresses this issue in the opening of *Isth*. 2; see 89. For an unsympathetic portrayal of Pindar as a "toady," see M. I. Finley, "Silver Tongue," in *Aspects of Antiquity* (New York: Penguin, 1977), 43–47.

22. The story of Kastor and Polydeukes is told at length in *Nem*. 10; see 112–13.

23. See Bundy, *Studia Pindarica*, 35–92.

24. For death as a motive for heroic action, see 56, 63.

25. For a discussion of the problems involved and a plausible reconstruction of the performance, see J. B. Lidov, "The Poems and Performance of Isthmians 3 and 4," *California Studies in Classical Antiquity* 7 (1975): 175–85.

26. For an excellent analysis of this poem, see D. C. Young, *Pindar Isthmian 7: Myth and Exempla* (Leiden, 1971).

27. For the holding back of essential items for climactic effect, see 26.

28. Bellerophon performs what was known as an "incubation"; that is, he slept on the altar of Athene. Typically Pindaric is the fact that Bellerophon's success depends upon a combination of human effort and divine aid.

29. For a brief analysis of the catalog in *Isth*. 7, see 108–9. The organization of the catalog in *Nem*. 10 is very different and it ends with Herakles' marriage to Heba, a motif that ended *Nem*. 1.

30. The Tyndarids are regularly portrayed as enjoying athletic banquets, as in the anecdote about Simonides who was saved from the collapsing house by them (see 25 with n. 15). *Ol*. 3 also involves *theoxenia* (feastings for gods) for the Tyndarids.

31. Diagoras' victories are listed on 19–20. For a close analysis of this ode, particularly of its imagery from nature, see Young, *Three Odes of Pindar*, 69–105.

32. The mule-cart race was held at Olympia from 500 to 444 B.C. It had so little prestige that it was not even included among the events on the Oxyrhynchus papyrus list of Olympic victors. *Ol*. 5 to Psaumis of Kamarina (in Sicily) is the only other ode for a victor in the mule race. Aristotle (*Rhet*. 3.2) tells an amusing anecdote about Simonides in order to illustrate how choice of words can portray a subject in a good or bad light. "When the victor in a mule race offered him a small commission, he refused to write the poem with the excuse that it was beneath him to write about mules; but when he gave the poet enough money, he wrote: 'Hail, daughters of storm-footed horses'; but of course they are also the daughters of asses."

33. Gildersleeve, *Pindar*, 171–72.

34. For a brief analysis, see 31.

35. See L. Woodbury, "Apollo's First Love. Pindar, *Pyth.* 9.26 ff.," *Transactions of the American Philological Association* 103 (1972): 561–73 and "Cyrene and the *Teleuta* of Marriage in Pindar's Ninth Pythian Ode," *Transactions of the American Philological Association* 112 (1982): 245–58.

36. For a translation and analysis of the hymn, see 28.

37. See Bundy, *Studia Pindarica*, 1–33. He proves that there is no foundation for the view of many commentators that the shorter ode is the "interest" on the debt mentioned in *Ol.* 10. Some earlier editions incorrectly reverse the order of these two odes.

38. For the "essential information" in this poem, see 26. For two interesting studies of this ode, see P. J. Nassen, "A Literary Study of Pindar's *Olympian* 10," *Transactions of the American Philological Association* 105 (1975): 219–40, and G. Kromer, "The Value of Time in Pindar's *Olympian* 10," *Hermes* 104 (1976): 420–36.

Chapter Seven

1. For a brief survey of lyric poetry after Pindar, see A. Lesky, *A History of Greek Literature*, trans J. Willis and C. de Heer (New York: Crowell, 1966), 413–417.

2. The most famous Pindaric quotation in Plato is spoken by Kallikles in the *Gorgias* (484B): "Law (*nomos*) is the king of all . . .," and it has been the subject of considerable interest, especially since the discovery of additional fragments on papyri. See M. Ostwald, "Pindar, Nomos, and Heracles," *Harvard Studies in Classical Philology* 69 (1965): 109–38; C. O. Pavese, "The New Heracles Poem of Pindar," *Harvard Studies in Classical Philology* 72 (1967): 47–88; and H. Lloyd-Jones, "Pindar Fr. 169," *Harvard Studies in Classical Philology* 76 (1972): 45–56.

3. See Jaeger, "The Prince's Education," in *Paideia*, 3:84–105. For Isokrates' important place in the long tradition of counsel and praise for leaders, see the works of Born and Rewa, above, chap. 4, n. 41.

4. For Pindaric elements in Kallimachos's hymns see Bundy, "The 'Quarrel Between Kallimachos and Apollonios,'" and M. Poliakoff, "Nectar, Springs, and the Sea: Critical Terminology in Pindar and Callimachus," *Zeitschrift für Papyrologie und Epigraphik* 39 (1980): 41–47. For a text of the new epinician for Berenike, see *Supplementum Hellenisticum*, ed. H. Lloyd-Jones and P. Parsons (Berlin: de Gruyter, 1983), 100–110, and for a commentary see P. J. Parsons, "Callimachus: Victoria Berenices," *Zeitschrift für Papyrologie und Epigraphik* 25 (1977): 1–50.

5. For a good analysis of the encomiastic background of *Idyll* 16 to Hieron II (not to be confused with the Hieron of two centuries earlier that Pindar praised), see N. Austin, "Idyll 16: Theocritus and Simonides," *Transactions of the American Philological Association* 98 (1967): 1–21.

6. The preference for the smaller, detachable showpiece is characteristic of Theokritos and of the Hellenistic age generally. For a detailed comparison of *Idyll* 24 and Pindar's *Nem.* 1, see J. Stern, "Theocritus' *Idyll* 24," *American Journal of Philology* 95 (1974): 348–61.

7. For a thorough study of Pindaric elements in Horace, see E. L. Highbarger, "The Pindaric Style of Horace," *Transactions of the American Philological Association* 66 (1935): 222–55. See also G. Davis, "Silence and Decorum: Encomiastic Convention and the Epilogue of Horace *Carm.* 3.2," *Classical Antiquity* 2 (1983): 9–26.

8. See 67. Horace has interestingly reversed Pindar's order to man, hero, and god. In the remainder of the poem he proceeds in the opposite order, ending up with the man, Augustus.

9. For an analysis of this ode and of its debt to Pindar, see Fraenkel, *Horace*, 426–32.

10. See chap. 4, n. 21.

11. Cowley, for example, leaves off the second half of the poem in his adaptation entitled "The Praise of Pindar."

12. For a brief survey of Augustan literary conventions, see S. Commager, *The Odes of Horace: A Critical Study* (Bloomington: Indiana University Press, 1967), 31–49; for an analysis of the ode itself, see 59–65.

13. For a detailed list of poems and passages in Horace that are *recusationes*, see W. H. Race, "*Odes* 1.20: An Horatian *Recusatio*," *California Studies in Classical Antiquity* 11 (1978): 179–96, with the appendix.

14. Quintilian says that Horace is practically the only Latin lyric poet worth reading (*Institutio Oratoria* 10.1.96).

15. "Longinus" 33.5. It is very interesting that "Longinus" makes this point about Sophokles as well as Pindar, but only in the latter case did it become a conventional criticism.

16. The following brief sketch can be supplemented by these works: R. Shafer, *The English Ode to 1660* (Princeton: Princeton University Press, 1918); G. N. Shuster, *The English Ode from Milton to Keats* (New York: Columbia University Press, 1940); J. Heath-Stubbs, *The Ode* (Oxford: Oxford University Press, 1969); J. D. Jump, *The Ode* (London: Methuen, 1974); D. M. Robinson, *Pindar: A Poet of Eternal Ideas* (Baltimore: Johns Hopkins University Press, 1936); G. Highet, *The Classical Tradition* (Oxford: Oxford University Press, 1949); and R. A. Swanson, *Pindar's Odes* (Indianapolis, 1974), 215–59.

17. For a very thorough, but unsympathetic, treatment of Ronsard's borrowings, see I. Silver, *The Pindaric Odes of Ronsard* (Paris, 1937).

18. See Shafer, *The English Ode to 1660*, 72–78.

19. For a description of Milton's text of Pindar, see Robinson, *Pindar*, 26–27. For Cowley's use of Benedictus, see D. C. Allen, "Cowley's Pindar," *Modern Language Notes* 63 (1948): 184–85.

20. For an appreciation of the complexity of the ode, particularly of the

subtle effects of its language, see R. S. Peterson, *Imitation and Praise in the Poems of Ben Jonson* (New Haven: Yale University Press, 1981), 195–232.

21. For a good overview of Cowley's Pindaric imitations, see J. G. Taaffe, *Abraham Cowley* (New York: Twayne, 1972), 60–74. For a stimulating analysis of the theory behind the odes, particularly in relation to Hobbes's philosophy, see D. Trotter, *The Poetry of Abraham Cowley* (Totowa, N.J.: Rowman & Littlefield, 1979), 109–42.

22. See William Congreve, "A Discourse on the Pindarique Ode," in *The Complete Works of William Congreve*, ed. M. Summers (New York: Russell & Russell, 1964), 4:82–86. Interestingly, Congreve's "Discourse" is much better known than the Pindarique Ode it introduced.

23. For evaluations more sympathetic to Cowley's intentions, see A. H. Nethercot, "The Relation of Cowley's 'Pindarics' to Pindar's Odes," *Modern Philology* 19 (1921): 107–9, and H. D. Goldstein, "*Anglorum Pindarus*: Model and Milieu," *Comparative Literature* 17 (1965): 299–310.

24. For a translation and analysis of this passage, see 33. Cowley's "Resurrection" was probably his most famous and influential Pindarique ode.

25. Modern readers have become so used to poetry that is organized by such metaphors and images, that they tend to read them into Pindar's poems. The most ardent attempt is by G. Norwood, *Pindar* (Berkeley, 1945).

26. Voltaire later took up the cause of Perrault with his famous lines addressed to Pindar (at the beginning of ode 17):

> Toi [Pindar] qui possédas le talent
> De parler beaucoup sans rien dire;
> Toi qui modulas savamment
> Des vers que personne n'entend,
> Et qu'il faut toujours qu'on admire.

You who possessed the talent for saying much without saying anything; you who cleverly composed verses that no one understands, but which one must always admire.

27. In 1747 William Collins published "Odes on Several Descriptive and Allegoric Subjects," which contained both "Horatian" and "Pindaric" types. The Pindaric odes ("To Fear," "On the Poetical Character," "To Mercy," and "To Liberty") are loose adaptations of Pindaric form, including the curious order of strophe-epode-antistrophe in two of them. For a brief survey of the qualities the eighteenth century expected in a "Pindarick ode," see O. F. Sigworth, *William Collins* (New York: Twayne, 1965), 65–70.

28. The allusions in these two odes were so recondite that Gray was finally forced to add extensive notes in 1768. For the works of Gray and Collins, see R. Lonsdale, *The Poems of Gray, Collins, and Goldsmith* (New York: Longman, 1969). A delightful parody of the eighteenth-century Pindaric ode

entitled "An Ode, Secundum Artem" (1763) is (doubtfully) attributed to William Cowper. Its opening lines reveal the emotional heightening expected in such productions:

> Shall I begin with *Ah*, or *Oh?*
> Be sad? *Oh!* yes. Be glad? *Ah!* no.
> Light subjects suit not grave Pindaric ode,
> Which walks in metre down the Strophic road. . . .

29. For a detailed overview of the eighteenth-century notion of the "sublime" and of the place of the Pindaric ode in it, see S. H. Monk, *The Sublime: A Study of Critical Theories in XVIII-Century England* (New York: Modern Language Assoc., 1935). Given such conceptions of elevated and sublime poetry, it is easy to see why the occasional nature of Pindaric odes—the fact that they were written to athletes and kings on commission—became more and more of an embarrassment that had to be excused or overlooked. Pindar's odes were increasingly read as a series of "purple patches."

30. Highet, *The Classical Tradition*, 251, calls Wordsworth's ode "the greatest modern Pindaric poem." His entire chapter, "The Renaissance and Afterwards: Lyric Poetry," 219–54, fills in many poets not covered here.

31. For the complex relationship of Hölderlin and Pindar, see R. B. Harrison, "Pindar," in *Hölderlin and Pindar* (Oxford: Oxford University Press, 1975), 279–301.

Selected Bibliography

PRIMARY SOURCES

1. Editions of the Greek text

Boeckh, A. *Pindari opera quae supersunt.* 2 vols. Leipzig: Weigel, 1811–21. A landmark in Pindaric scholarship, this edition reconstituted the longer line units ("periods") that more clearly reflect the structure and sense of Pindar's verse. The commentary (in Latin) is still very useful.

Bowra, C. M. *Pindari Carmina cum Fragmentis.* 2d. ed. Oxford: Oxford University Press, 1947. The Oxford Classical Text of Pindar.

Puech, A. *Pindare.* 4 vols. Paris: Les Belles Lettres, 1922–23. Frequently reprinted. The French Budé text of Pindar with extensive introductions and facing French translation.

Sandys, J. E. *The Odes of Pindar.* 2d ed. rev. Cambridge, Mass.: Harvard University Press, 1937. The Loeb Classical Library edition with facing translation in English. With the exception of its archaic English and numerous small errors, this is a good working edition. It includes translations of the principal fragments.

Snell, B. and Maehler, H. *Pindarus.* 2 vols. Leipzig: Teubner, 1971. Subsequent printings contain revisions. Volume 1 contains the epinician odes, volume 2 the fragments. This has become the standard text for Pindar.

Turyn, A. *Pindari Carmina cum Fragmentis.* Oxford: Blackwell, 1952. A good edition, beautifully printed.

2. Commentaries

Bury J. B. *The Isthmian Odes of Pindar.* 1892. (Reprint. Amsterdam: Hakkert, 1965).

———. *The Nemean Odes of Pindar.* 1890. (Reprint. Amsterdam: Hakkert, 1965). Very erratic commentaries.

Carey, C. *A Commentary on Five Odes of Pindar, Pythian 2, Pythian 9, Nemean 1, Nemean 7, Isthmian 8.* New York: Arno Press, 1981. A detailed commentary on these important and often difficult odes.

Farnell, L. R. *Works of Pindar.* Vol. 2. *Critical Commentary.* London: Macmillan, 1932. A provocative, uneven commentary.

Fennell, C. A. M. *The Nemean and Isthmian Odes.* New ed. Cambridge: Cambridge University Press, 1899.

————. *Pindar: The Olympian and Pythian Odes.* New ed. Cambridge: Cambridge University Press, 1893. Somewhat dated, but still very useful commentaries.

Gildersleeve, B. L. *Pindar: The Olympian and Pythian Odes.* 1885. Reprint. Harborview, N.Y.: Arno, 1979. A very good commentary by the doyen of American Pindarists.

Hamilton, R. *Pindar: Selected Odes.* Bryn Mawr: Bryn Mawr Commentaries, 1985. A reading commentary for advanced students of Greek on eleven odes.

Kirkwood, G. *Selections from Pindar.* Chico, Calif.: Scholars Press, 1982. Excellent introduction with up to date commentary on seventeen odes and *Paian 6.*

Radt, S. L. *Pindars zweiter and sechster Paian.* Amsterdam: Hakkert, 1958. The standard commentary on the two most important paians.

Thummer, E. *Pindar: Die Isthmischen Gedichte.* 2 vols. Heidelberg: Winter, 1968–69. The first volume is an overall analysis of motifs in the odes, the second is a commentary on the Isthmian odes.

3. Translations

Bowra, C. M. *Pindar: The Odes.* New York: Penguin, 1969. Generally readable. The notes contain many doubtful historical references.

Conway, G. S. *The Odes of Pindar.* London: Dent & Sons, 1972. This edition provides helpful information and a readable translation.

Lattimore, R. *The Odes of Pindar.* Chicago: University of Chicago Press, 1947. Translation very obscure at points, few notes, useful glossary.

Nisetich, F. J. *Pindar's Victory Odes.* Baltimore: The Johns Hopkins Univ. Pr., 1980. The clearest and most accurate translation in English. Excellent general introduction and prefaces to each ode.

Ruck, C. A. P. and Matheson, W. H. *Pindar. Selected Odes.* Ann Arbor: Univ. of Michigan Pr., 1968. Free translations of eighteen odes with uneven interpretative essays.

Swanson, R. A. *Pindar's Odes.* Indianapolis: Bobbs-Merrill, 1974. Translation obscure at points, helpful introduction and notes, a chapter on Pindaric imitations with examples.

4. Lexical and Bibliographical aids

Drachmann, A. B. *Scholia Vetera in Pindari Carmina.* 3 vols. Leipzig: Teubner, 1903–27. The standard edition of the ancient scholia. No translation is provided.

Gerber, D. E. *A Bibliography of Pindar 1513–1966.* Philological Monographs of the American Philogical Association. vol. 28. Cleveland: Case Western Reserve Press, 1969.

————. *Emendations in Pindar 1513–1972.* Amsterdam: Hakkert, 1976. A

convenient catalog of emendations (corrections) proposed since the first
printed edition.

————. "Pindar," *Studies in Greek Lyric Poetry 1967–1975*, special issue of
Classical World 70 (1976): 132–57. A continuation of his *Bibliography of
Pindar*, but with annotations.

Irigoin, J. *Histoire du Texte de Pindare*. Paris: Librairie C. Klincksieck, 1952.
A detailed and interesting study of Pindar's text from the beginning to
the first printed editions.

Slater, W. J. *Lexicon to Pindar*. Berlin: de Gruyter, 1969. An indispensable
aid for reading Pindar in Greek.

Young, D. C. "Pindaric Criticism." *Minnesota Review* 4 (1964): 584–641.
Reprinted in *Pindaros und Bacchylides*, edited by W. M. Calder III and J.
Stern. *Wege der Forschung*, vol. 134. Darmstadt: Wissenschaftliche Buch-
gesellschaft, 1970. A review of nineteenth and twentieth-century criticism, particularly on the problem of unity in the odes.

SECONDARY SOURCES

Bowra, C. M. *Pindar*. Oxford: Oxford University Press, 1964. A wide-ranging, eclectic book.

Bundy, E. L. "The 'Quarrel Between Kallimachos and Apollonios,' Part I:
The Epilogue of Kallimachos's *Hymn to Apollo*." *California Studies in Classical Antiquity* 5 (1972): 39–94. Contains many important brief observations on Pindaric passages and supplements *Studia Pindarica*.

————. *Studia Pindarica*. 2 vols. University of California Publications in
Classical Philology. vol. 18. Berkeley: University of California Press,
1962. Detailed analyses of *Ol.* 11 and *Isth.* 1. Difficult to read but a
landmark in establishing the poetic and rhetorical conventions in the
odes.

Burton, R. W. B. *Pindar's Pythian Odes*. Oxford: Oxford University Press,
1962. A careful and often insightful analysis of the twelve *Pythian* odes.

Carne-Ross, D. S. *Pindar*. New Haven: Yale University Press, 1985. A sensitive analysis of twelve odes, "written to convey to the general reader
the skill and power of Pindar's poetry."

Crotty, K. *Song and Action: The Victory Odes of Pindar*. Baltimore: Johns Hopkins University Press, 1982. A wide-ranging discussion of aspects of
Pindar's odes.

Finley, J. H., Jr. *Pindar and Aeschylus*. Cambridge, Mass.: Harvard University Press, 1955. Combines historical and literary ("symbolic") approaches to Pindar.

Finley, M. I. and Pleket, H. W. *The Olympic Games: The First Thousand Years*.
New York: Viking, 1976. An excellent overview of the Olympic games.

Fränkel, H. "Pindar and Bacchylides." In *Early Greek Poetry and Philosophy,* translated by M. Hadas and J. Willis, 425–504. Oxford: Blackwell, 1975. A stimulating discussion of various aspects of Pindar.

Gerber, D. E. *Pindar's Olympian One: A Commentary.* Phoenix Supplement, no. 15. Toronto: University of Toronto Press, 1982. A full-scale commentary on this single ode.

Greengard, C. *The Structure of Pindar's Epinician Odes.* Amsterdam: Hakkert, 1980. A study of formal patterns on various levels (meter, language, theme) in Pindar's odes.

van Groningen, B. A. *La Composition littéraire archaïque grecque.* Amsterdam: Noord-Hollandsche Uitgevers Maatschappij, 1958, 324–86. An analysis of ring-composition and narrative form in eight odes.

Hamilton, R. *Epinikion: General Form in the Odes of Pindar.* The Hague: Mouton, 1974. An analysis of the organization of an ode's "parts."

Jaeger, W. "Pindar and the Voice of the Aristocracy." In *Paideia,* translated by G. Highet, 1:205–22. 3 vols. Oxford: Oxford University Press, 1945. An overview of the educational aims of Pindar's odes.

Jebb, R. C. *Bacchylides: The Poems and Fragments.* Cambridge: Cambridge University Press, 1905. Still the standard commentary in English of Pindar's contemporary epinician poet.

———. "Pindar." *Journal of Hellenic Studies* 3 (1882):144–93. An overview of various aspects of Pindar.

Köhnken, A. *Die Funktion des Mythos bei Pindar.* Berlin: de Gruyter, 1971. A Study of Pindar's use of myth in six odes (*Pyth.* 10, 12; *Nem.* 4, 7, 8; and *Isth.* 4).

Lefkowitz, M. R. *The Lives of the Greek Poets.* Baltimore: Johns Hopkins University Press, 1981. A study of the ancient biographers' methods. Contains a chapter on Pindar and a translation of the Vita Ambrosiana.

———. "*Tō Kai Egō*: The First Person in Pindar." *Harvard Studies in Classical Philology* 67 (1963): 177–253. A study of "I" and "we" in the odes as they relate to the poet.

———. *The Victory Ode: An Introduction.* Park Ridge, N. J.: Noyes, 1976. A close analysis of Pindar's and Bacchylides' odes to Hieron.

Lloyd-Jones, H. "Modern Interpretation of Pindar: The Second Pythian and Seventh Nemean Odes." *Journal of Hellenic Studies* 93 (1973): 109–37. The first nine pages provide a survey of recent trends in Pindaric scholarship.

Mullen, W. *Choreia: Pindar and Dance.* Princeton: Princeton University Press, 1982. A study of ancient dance and its relationship to the form and content of the odes.

Newman, J. K. and Newman, F. S. *Pindar's Art: Its Tradition and Aims.* Munich: Weidemann, 1984. Offers a "new approach" to Pindar's epinicians. It contains a brief survey of nineteenth-century scholarship and analyses of seventeen odes, with emphasis on the role of the *kōmos* (festive celebration) in the odes and Pindar's use of verbal and metrical repetition.

Norwood, G. *Pindar.* Berkeley: University of California Press, 1945. A learned, stimulating study that attempts to interpret the odes through "symbolism."

Podlecki, A. J. *The Early Greek Poets and Their Times.* Vancouver: University of British Columbia Press, 1984. The chapter on Pindar and Bacchylides owes much to Bowra, but is more cautious in detecting historical allusions in the odes.

Yalouris, N. ed. *The Eternal Olympics.* New Rochelle, N.Y.: Caratzas, 1979. Good collection of plates illustrating Greek athletics.

Young, D. C. "Pindar." In *Ancient Writers*, edited by J. T. Luce, 1:157–77. New York: Scribner's, 1982. A general overview of Pindar's work.

———. *Pindar Isthmian 7: Myth and Exempla.* Mnemosyne Supplement, no. 15. Leiden: Brill, 1971. A literary study of *Isth. 7.*

———. *Three Odes of Pindar: A Literary Study of Pythian 11, Pythian 3, and Olympian 7.* Mnemosyne Supplement, no. 9. Leiden: Brill, 1968. A basic study of these three odes.

Index